Parents Ask, Experts Answer:

Nurturing Happy, Healthy Children

Tina Nocera

Bulk Purchase

Gryphon House books are available for special premiums and sales promotions as well as for fund-raising use. Special editions or book excerpts also can be created to specifications. For details, contact the Director of Marketing at Gryphon House.

Disclaimer

Gryphon House, Inc. cannot be held responsible for damage, mishap, or injury incurred during the use of or because of activities in this book. Appropriate and reasonable caution and adult supervision of children involved in activities and corresponding to the age and capability of each child involved are recommended at all times. Do not leave children unattended at any time. Observe safety and caution at all times.

We do not provide medical advice. The information contained in the Parental Wisdom® website and this book provides a vehicle for parents and caregivers to choose advice that best fits their child and situation. This is not a substitute for professional advice. If you have questions or concerns regarding the physical or mental health of your child, please seek assistance from a qualified healthcare provider.

Parents Ask, Experts Answer

Nurturing Happy, Healthy Children

Eating

Sleeping

Potty Problems

Bullies

Peer Pressure

Tantrums

Sibling Rivalry

Manners

Caregiving

Education

Tina Nocera

Gryphon House, Inc.
Lewisville, NC

Copyright

© 2014 Tina Nocera

Published by Gryphon House, Inc.

P. O. Box 10, Lewisville, NC 27023

800.638.0928; 877.638.7576 (fax)

Visit us on the web at www.gryphonhouse.com.

Parental Wisdom® uses methods for answering child-development questions patented by Tina Nocera, numbers 6,193,518 and 6,482,012.

Cover photograph courtesy of Shutterstock Photography, www.shutterstock.com © 2013.

Library of Congress Cataloging-in-Publication Data

The Cataloging-in-Publication Data is registered with the Library of Congress for ISBN: 978-0-87659-022-5.

Table of Contents

Contributor Biographies

Tina Nocera founded Parental Wisdom® after struggling to find answers to her parenting questions. Tina noticed that, although she found an overwhelming amount of information, she couldn't find answers that gave parents a choice. It was like trying to take a drink of water from a fire hose; a person could drown and still be left thirsty. While past generations relied on extended family support systems for parenting help, today's mobile families deal with increased societal issues, cultural diversity, and powerful media and marketing influences. The questions and challenges are more complex, so a single answer from a single expert may not work for all parents. Parental Wisdom lets parents ask questions and receive multiple answers from trusted advisors, so the parents can decide which response is the most appropriate for their unique child and situation.

Tina created and served as editor-in-chief of Viewpoints on Parenting, a national publication for Toys "R" Us. She is the author of *Because Kids Don't Come with Manuals*® and created the Good Parenting Seal℠ to help parents evaluate books and CDs. She has presented seminars on Project Imagine!®, a program for middle-school students and their parents; audio broadcasts for the Park Bench® discussion forum; and has created the Happy Tears® merchandise and card line. She has written the Parental Wisdom blog since 2006. Tina has a bachelor of arts degree and master of business administration degree from Chadwick University. She serves as the director of global ecommerce, strategy, and business development for Toys "R" Us.

She lives in New Jersey with her husband, Mike. Her son, Michael, is serving in the U.S. Army, and her daughter, Noelle, works in public relations and lives in New York. Their family's favorite thing to do is to have dinner together when everyone is in town.

Brenda Bercun is a pediatric nurse practitioner, a clinical nurse specialist in child and family mental health, and the author of *I'm Going to Be a Big Brother!* and *I'm Going to Be a Big Sister!* Her website is www.nurturingyourchildren.com.

Trish Booth, MA, is an author, educator, and grandmother. She taught her first childbirth class in 1972. Since then, she has focused on providing supportive education on pregnancy and parenting topics. She has developed classes; created more than seventy-five pamphlets, including the *Staying Positive while Parenting* series; and written several books, including *Pregnancy Q&A*. Trish has trained pre- and postnatal educators, nurses, and doulas in family-centered care and infant competencies. Currently, she is a medical education process consultant and web editor. She delights in being Gram to her five grandchildren.

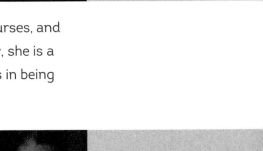

Mark J. Borowski, MS, is a speaker and coach in the areas of leadership and parenting. He started his own business, The Learning Interface, in 1999, when his first daughter was born, so he could be a part-time at-home dad. His experience with his children inspired him to publish *Big Slick Daddy: Poker Strategies for Parenting Success* in 2007, utilizing the language and strategies of poker to connect with dads in a unique way. His book was awarded the Good Parenting Seal from Parental Wisdom, where he contributes as an advisor and helps parents meet their daily challenges.

He continues to enjoy his corporate work in leadership development as well as his work with parents. He understands the similarities between the roles and believes that great leadership with a lasting legacy starts in the home. His websites are found at www.NewLookOfLeadership.com and www.BigSlickDaddy.com.

Charlotte Cowan, MD, is a board-certified pediatrician. She trained at and practiced for many years at Boston's Massachusetts General Hospital (MGH) for Children, where she remains on staff. During her clinical years at MGH, she served on the faculty of Harvard Medical School. Additionally, Dr. Cowan has completed a fellowship in medical ethics at the University of Chicago and is a current fellow of the American Academy of Pediatrics. Find her website at www.drhippo.com.

Naomi Drew is recognized around the world for her work in conflict resolution and peacemaking. She is the award-winning author of several books, including *No Kidding About Bullying*. Her book *Learning the Skills of Peacemaking* was one of the first to introduce peacemaking into public education. Her work has enabled families, educators, and children to live these skills on a daily basis. Her website is located at www.learningpeace.com.

Georgianna Duarte, PhD, is a professor in the department of teaching, learning, and innovation at the University of Texas, Brownsville. Her research areas include language and play in bilingual environments, language and outdoor play, mentoring, and curriculum in international settings. She teaches courses in curriculum in early childhood education; parent, family, and community partnerships; and early childhood environments.

Ellen Gibran-Hesse is a parent educator, life coach, attorney, and single mother.

Barbara Gilmour is the creator and executive director of Cool Kind Kid, the developer of Cool Kind Kid social skills and anti-bullying educational materials. She was raised in a family where good social skills were taught and practiced. She has a bachelor of science degree from Pennsylvania State University, where she also received etiquette instruction. In the mid-1990s, she spent a year researching and writing two ten-hour courses, Manners for Kids 8–12 and Manners for Teens. She started a business teaching these courses locally and spent several years expanding the content of the courses for younger children to include character values, anti-bullying materials, and the Cool Kind Kid concept. This content has been incorporated into the Tanner's Manners: Be a Cool Kind Kid music and educational materials for elementary-age children. Her materials help children learn to reject bullying and equip them with the social skills needed for successful futures. Visit her website at www.coolkindkid.com.

Sally Goldberg, PhD, is a Cornell graduate and specialist in the field of early childhood education. She has been helping parents and teachers for many years. As a professor of education, Dr. Sally branched out to become an author and a frequent guest on TV and radio. She now focuses her energy daily online at Parenting Tips with Dr. Sally, www.earlychildhoodnews.net/parenting-tips.

Ilyse M. Gorbunoff, MS, is a pre-K and kindergarten curriculum coach and has been an educator for more than thirty years. She believes that passion is the key ingredient to being a successful educator. She relishes opportunities to encourage and support other teachers so that they can bring the same excitement and dedication to their students.

She and her husband have raised three wonderful, strong, independent, and kind young men. She is proud of them each and every day and is excited to share some of what she has learned along the way.

Dr. Tom Greenspon is a psychologist, marriage and family therapist, and author. He earned a bachelor of arts degree from Yale and a PhD in psychology from the University of Illinois. After a postdoctoral fellowship at the University of Rochester, he joined the faculty of the medical center at the University of Alabama at Birmingham, where he was involved in teaching, research, and counseling.

Tom lectures and writes on a variety of topics, including couples' and family relationships and the emotional needs of gifted children and adults. He is a member of several professional organizations, has authored a monograph on adolescent-adult relationships for the Unitarian Universalist Association, and a number of his articles have appeared in professional journals. His first book, *Freeing Our Families from Perfectionism*, has won the National Parenting Publications Gold Award and a Parents' Choice Award.

Ashley Hammond is the founder and owner of Sports Domain Academy (SDA). His love for teaching the game of soccer has taken him all over the world, and he hopes to share his passion through SDA's dedication to excellence. See his website at www.sdamontclair.com.

Christine Hierlmaier Nelson is a writer and mother of two beautiful girls. Her pre-K children's book, *Green Yellow Go! Nat Knows Bananas*, teaches children about patience, time, and colors. Christine uses her training in communications to share with parents, early childhood educators, and child care providers why patience is a critical skill for raising and nurturing successful children. Her book and insights have been featured in *Parents* magazine, *Redbook*, *First for Women*, and on the BAM! radio network. Find her book and blog at www.patientparents.com.

Norman Hoffman, PhD, is a forensic mental health evaluator.

Dr. Steven Kairys is chairman of the department of pediatrics at the Jersey Shore University Medical Center.

Michelle P. Maidenberg, PhD, MPH, LCSW-R, CGP, is the president and clinical director of Westchester Group Works, www.WestchesterGroupWorks.com.

Jack Marcellus is president of The Focus Academy, www. thefocusacademy.com.

Aileen McCabe-Maucher is the author of *The Inner Peace Diet*. She is a licensed clinical social worker and psychotherapist who has helped many people find inner peace and discover their unique life purposes. Aileen has worked for more than fifteen years to provide individual and group counseling to a diverse client population. She is a graduate of West Chester University, Widener University, the University of Delaware, and the Gestalt Therapy Institute of Philadelphia at Bryn Mawr College. Aileen is a registered yoga teacher with Yoga Alliance. She is currently pursuing a doctorate at the University of Pennsylvania and is writing her third book. Visit Aileen's website at www.theinnerpeacediet.com.

Brenda Nixon, MA, is a parenting speaker and author. She empowers audiences with information and affirmation on child rearing. Visit her blog at www.BrendaNixonOnParenting. blogspot.com.

Dr. Vicki Panaccione is an internationally recognized child psychologist, parenting expert, speaker, parent coach, media specialist, consultant, author, and radio personality. She has dedicated her career to working with hundreds of children and helping thousands of parents raise happy, successful kids. Dr. Vicki is the author of *What Kids Would Tell You . . . If Only You'd Ask!* and *Your Child's Inner Brilliance.* She is frequently quoted in publications such as *The New York Times*, *Parents*, *Parenting*, and *Woman's Day*, as well as on websites such as Newsday, Good Housekeeping, Forbes, WebMD, iParenting, and Love to Know. She is featured on a weekly parenting show on Heartbeat Radio for Women and serves as a parenting consultant for ParentalWisdom.com and Nickelodeon's ParentsConnect.com. She is proudest of being Alex's mom. Her son graduated from Emory University and is currently a graduate student at Vanderbilt University, doing cancer research at Yale University toward his doctorate in cancer biology.

Janet Price, MEd, MA, has clinical experience working with children, adolescents, adults, couples, and families. Before choosing a career in clinical psychology, Janet worked for more than thirty years in the fields of early childhood and special needs. Visit www.vpa-psychologist.com/Psychologists.html.

Elinor Robin, PhD, is a Florida Supreme Court–certified mediator and mediation trainer. Her area of expertise is professional and personal relationship conflict, especially in divorce, family estrangement, the workplace, and business partnership. She earned a PhD in psychology with a

specialization in conflict management and is licensed as both a mental health counselor and marriage and family therapist. Over the last twenty-four years, Elinor has taught mediation to more than twelve thousand professionals and has mediated thousands of disputes. She is a member of the Florida Supreme Court's mediator qualifications board, a contract mediator with the U.S. Postal Service's REDRESS Mediation Program, a past president of the Association of South Florida Mediators and Arbitrators, executive vice president of Mediation Training Group, Inc., and a lead mediator with A Friendly Divorce, Inc. She has been quoted in *The Wall Street Journal*, *NY Daily News*, FoxBusiness.com, CNN.com, Entrepreneur.com, and various other media. Visit www.ElinorRobin.com, www.AFriendlyDivorce.com, or www.MediationTrainingGroup.com to learn more.

Rosalind Sedacca, CCT, is the founder of the Child-Centered Divorce Network, where parents can access her free articles, ezine, blog, coaching services, and other valuable resources to help them create the most positive outcome for their family before, during, and after divorce. She is the author of *How Do I Tell the Kids about the Divorce? A Create-a-Storybook Guide to Preparing Your Children—With Love!* Visit www.childcentereddivorce.com to learn more.

Amy Sherman is a therapist, author, seminar facilitator, and licensed mental health counselor focusing on the issues related to the population of adults over forty, including dealing with adolescents and teens and young-adult children. Visit her website at www.bummedoutboomer.com.

Sharon Silver helps parents bridge the gap between the logical adult world, the emotional world of children, and the reality of everyday life. She is a parent educator and has been a facilitator for The Cline Fay Institute and Redirecting Children's Behavior programs. She is the author of *Stop Reacting and Start Responding: 108 Ways to Discipline Consciously and Become the Parent You Want to Be*. She contributes to http://askmoxie.org and www.themomentrepreneur.com. Learn more at www.proactiveparenting.net.

Eleanor P. Taylor, MS, has spent her nursing career in preventive medicine, including twenty years as director of a hospital-based wellness center. She holds a masters degree in family health nursing and has national certifications as a diabetes educator, lifestyle counselor, and health education specialist. Her main focus has been on nutrition and lifestyle modification. Ellie is the co-author of two books: *Feeding the Kids: The Flexible, No-Battles, Healthy Eating System for the Whole Family* and *Feeding the Kids Workshops: Raising Happy, Healthy Eaters*. She lives in Clemson, South Carolina. Visit her website at www.FeedingTheKids.com.

Jim Taylor, PhD, is an internationally recognized authority on the psychology of performance. He works with CEOs and senior management of companies around the world, professional and world-class athletes, and other high achievers.

Mark D. Viator, PhD, LPC-S, is a licensed and nationally certified counselor.

Penny Warner has published more than sixty books for adults and children. She holds a bachelor's degree in child development and a master's degree in special education. She teaches child development at a local college and has appeared on television featuring ideas from her books, including the PBS series, *Parent Sense*, the *Later Today* show, HGTV, and dozens of others. She pens a weekly newspaper column on family life. She has two grown children and four grandchildren.

Pamela Waterman is president of Metal Mouth Media, home of the award-winning Braces Cookbooks blog, www. MetalMouthMedia.net/wired-in.

Janet Whalley, RN, IBCLC, is a nurse, lactation consultant, breastfeeding educator, and author. Her work has focused on helping new families since 1975, when she began teaching birth and breastfeeding classes. She teaches breastfeeding classes for Great Starts at Parent Trust and is a co-author of two books: *Pregnancy, Childbirth and the Newborn* and *The Simple Guide to Having a Baby*. Her work with Beyond Birth Seattle includes providing telephone counseling, teaching a Breastfeeding 911 class, and making home visits to help with breastfeeding problems. She enjoys working with new families and loves being a grandmother.

Derick Wilder is a dad; children's-book author; director for Playball, a child development organization; and founder of Reading Giraffe, a literacy initiative. Visit his website at www.DerickWilder.com.

Beverly Willett is a writer and mother of two. She has written for *The New York Times*, *Newsweek*, *Woman's Day*, *Family Circle*, *Prevention*, The Huffington Post, Salon.com, *Parenting*, and The Daily Beast, among others. She is a former contributing editor to *Chicken Soup for the Soul* magazine and has written articles for the Toys "R" Us publication *Viewpoints on Parenting*. She is co-chair of the Coalition for Divorce Reform and is currently at work on her first book. Before becoming a writer, Beverly practiced entertainment and copyright law in New York City. Visit her website at www.beverlywillett.com.

Jill Wodnick is a national speaker as a Lamaze childbirth educator, certified lactation counselor, and birth doula. She supports families through prenatal education, prenatal yoga, and the wonder of giving birth and being born. Blending public policy and interpersonal support, Jill works on health-equity topics and the role of doulas to reduce perinatal disparities through a task force for Medicaid coverage of doulas. Jill has taught undergraduates, graduate students, health professionals, and hundreds of expectant parents on evidence-based, mother-friendly, baby-friendly maternity care. She is part of the World Organization of Perinatal Educators seeking to prevent all forms of violence. Part of One Million Women Drumming, Jill lives in Montclair, New Jersey, with her family and can be found singing, drumming, baking, and playing board games. Visit her website at www.JillWodnick.com.

Introduction

Imagine a job more difficult and important than being the president of the United States, with ninety-one required skills, no formal training or feedback mechanism, and a never-ending supply of contradictory advice. Welcome to parenthood!

Other
Coach Artist
Teacher Mediator Barber Maid Entertainer
Farmer GateKeeper Librarian Repairer Zookeeper Ironing
Laundress Receptionist Mother Fundraiser MeterReader
HomeEconomist Advocate GriefCounselor Veterinarian Bookkeeper
FileClerk Restaurateur InteriorDesign FinancialPlanner Planner
Storyteller Environmentalist **Mom** VocationalCounselor Judge
YardMaintenance Philosopher EfficiencyExpert
SportsInstructor PhotoJournalist KitchenManager
RecreationalSpecialist HealthCareProvider EmergencyMedicalTechnician
RaisingConsciousness CrisisManagement Buyer
Statistician **Dad** ChildCareExpert CreativeDirector FurnitureUpholsterer Waitress
Referee Coach QuarrelSolver ValuesExpert FinderOfLostThings FoodShopper
Reporter EmotionalSupport Stargazer Cook
Plumber UrbanPlanner Mathematician WasteRemoval ProjectPlanner NutritionExpert Baker
SocialWorker Psychologist ShoeRepair Nurse Quartermaster Shopper
PianoTuner LetterCarrier DogGroomer Meteorologist Dietician
Dishwasher TravelAgent Party Sociologist X-rayVision Gardner
Typist Secretary Chef
Advisor Economist OfficeClerk Investor
TaxiDriver Paralegal
Electrician

BC (Before Children), we were observers, possibly believing parents lacked our level of organization and control. We were certain that when we became parents it would be different. Our children would be little angels, and we would not be the sleep- and shower-deprived, clueless people who allow three-year-olds to hold them hostage for a cookie. No, not us.

How could we have been so wrong?

When you become a parent, you assume other parents must have it all figured out, but there is no decoder ring or secret handshake. No matter how similar other children or situations may seem to your own, often they are not. Your unique child lives within your unique family and the values and culture you create. And, when you finally get to a comfort level of understanding with your first child, you find that the knowledge doesn't scale with your second as you thought it would. Each child is unique.

Most new (and experienced) parents get advice by asking their moms, friends, sisters, brothers, neighbors, doctors, or co-workers how to handle a situation.

> If you bungle raising your children, I don't think whatever else you do well matters very much.
> —Jacqueline Kennedy Onassis

That approach is flawed for a number of reasons:

- What if the person offering advice hasn't had experience with the situation you're dealing with? Our moms didn't raise us in the same media- and marketing-intense world that we face now.
- What if you don't agree with the advice that is offered? Relationships are often compromised when different parenting styles come to light.
- Will you have to report back to the person who offered advice? When does the conversation end? Can you guarantee your question won't be a topic of discussion with others?
- What if you talk with a professional but get advice that just doesn't feel right? Because that person has an advanced degree, does that mean she knows better than you do?
- Most important, what if your child does something you simply don't want to share? Now where can you go for advice?

When my own children were little, I read the books and realized that, even though experts had credentials and solid opinions based on research, I did not agree with a single expert's advice all the time. Recognizing the need for something different, something better, something tangible, I created Parental Wisdom™ because kids don't come with manuals™.

Parental Wisdom provides a patented method of offering advice from child-development experts in response to parent questions. Because parents know their children best, Parental Wisdom lets them choose the advice that best fits with their individual circumstances.

As Dr. Benjamin Spock famously said, "Trust yourself. You know more than you think you do." The Parental Wisdom concept gives parents confidence by offering the advice of multiple, caring, and trusted professionals. There may be several right answers and several ways to say something, but in the end, you have to be comfortable with the way you are handling a situation with your child. This book offers expert advice on a number of common parenting and child-development questions. Find the questions you are facing, and read the responses. Then, decide on the approach that works best for your child, your family, and your situation. We hope you find this book helpful on this wonderful journey called parenting.

Tina Nocera, Founder

Parental Wisdom®

www.parentalwisdom.com

Chapter 1

Daily Dilemmas:
Eating, Sleeping, and Potty Problems

Q My two-year-old daughter will sit with us at the table and eat—usually. Should I have her eat if she doesn't want to? Should I force her to try new foods? Should I make her sit there until her plate is clean or until she's eaten two bites of peas? If she asks to leave the table before her father and I are finished eating, do I let her?

Eleanor Taylor

Your daughter is probably too young to tolerate sitting at the table for long periods, and it's typical for two-year-olds to want to eat and go. Offer her small amounts of all the foods you are eating, and when she is done, happily excuse her from the table. You might want to include one of her favorite foods at each meal, if you know that she won't like anything else being served. The important thing is that she enjoys her experience eating at the table with the family and that she is not pressured to eat foods she does not like. Two-year-olds often eat small meals, with about 20 percent of their nutritional needs met by snacks. Plan a healthy snack schedule, so she will be hungry when she comes to the table for a meal.

Janet Price

Your question touches on one of the areas of parenting that can spark the most angst, frustration, and potential long-term challenges: our responsibility to make sure our child is healthy and on our values and traditions about meals. When two parents are involved, there are two sets of values and rituals influencing these decisions. At first glance, this arena may seem straightforward, but it is really quite complex. You are wise to be thinking about how you want to handle this now so that your daughter's eating time can be enjoyable, positive, and healthy. The number one goal is to make eating an enjoyable time. Provide as much calm and relaxation around mealtime as possible.

Two-year-olds need structure during eating time. Be consistent about when meals are served. A high chair or child chair can provide external boundaries that help them keep their bodies at the table. Toddlers also need caregivers to decide what and how much food is placed in front of them at one time. Your daughter is letting you know how much food she actually needs.

As far as keeping her at the table when she indicates her desire to leave, what is important here is for your daughter to begin to learn that eating happens at the table. When she gets down from her chair, her eating time is over. This consistent response from you will help her begin to pay attention to what her body is telling her about being full or still hungry. Young children can be easily distracted by things other than eating. It will undoubtedly take time for her to learn to recognize when she really is full and finished with her meal.

I do not recommend forcing young children to eat food they are refusing. It creates power struggles that can make eating time miserable for everyone and has no redeeming value. Developmentally, two-year-olds are experimenting with independence. So, trying to make your daughter eat provides her an opportunity to flex her newfound skill of saying no and to progress to a full-blown temper tantrum if her no is not respected.

Many of us were told to eat everything on our plates. Raising a child with the expectation of eating everything on her plate keeps her from noting when she is full. The practice can contribute to overeating, which then is likely to cause other food-related problems, such as difficulty in maintaining a healthy weight.

If your child chooses to leave the table while you and your husband are still eating, encourage her to have quiet, play-alone time while you finish your meal. If you have a play area near where you eat, she can play by herself until you are done. Your child's ability to play independently will affect how long you can continue once she has left the table.

Naomi Drew

I say absolutely no forcing. That's a no-win thing to do and only creates power struggles. Your best teaching tool is your good example and your ability to catch her in the act of doing things right. Offer her food, and encourage her to eat it. Praise her when she does, and tell her what a big girl she is. But, if she doesn't want to eat, let it be. Under no circumstances should you force her to sit there until her plate is clean. Doing so will make her dread mealtime and will make her resistant and resentful. Make mealtimes warm, pleasant, and loving.

In terms of leaving the table before you and her dad are finished, remember that she's only two. Have her sit there for a reasonable amount of time; then, tell her she's excused. In time, if mealtimes are pleasant and loving, she will be able to sit there for longer and longer periods. Try to find something at each meal to praise her for—using her fork, eating whatever she eats, or sitting nicely in her chair. Remember that sincere praise is far more powerful than threats and reprimands.

Q My toddler won't eat the same food as the rest of the family. How can I deal with that?

Pamela Waterman

Toddler-time is all about trying new things and asserting opinions. The common thought is that it can take ten tries before a child makes a decision about liking a new food. The texture, color, flavor, and temperature can all be different from what he's dealt with before, so it can just take patience and time. But, don't let that stop you from trying. Give the child one item that the rest of you are having—one new thing to try at each meal. Gradually transition from toddler foods as new foods are accepted. Some children will see what's on your plate and want it, just because they don't have it! As they get older, keep working at it, and praise them when they make progress.

As the child gets older, if he does not like what is served, he can always make a peanut-butter sandwich (assuming no allergies). Also, as he gets older, look at pictures of foods together and try recipes from cookbooks and magazines. In the grocery store, ask him if he sees something you could try together. And take heart—few children go to college these days only eating Cheerios.

Tina Nocera

I'm sure it won't help to say most parents have the same issue that you're dealing with when mealtimes are more about tantrums, screaming, and bribery than healthy eating. Fussy eating is a normal phase in your toddler's development. It will get better with time. Just try not to get anxious about it because it might make the problem worse.

Your toddler might not be able to take in all the calories you would like. His stomach is quite small, and he knows when he has had enough. There are obvious things you can do to get him to eat, such as not giving your child snacks too close to mealtimes and presenting bite-size foods in small containers. Don't worry so much about what your toddler eats in a day. Instead, think about what your toddler eats over a week.

Ilyse Gorbunoff

The most important thing to do is to try not to make food a battle. What worked for me is to be sure to have a family dinner each night. If you eat together, your toddler will be exposed to many foods and everyone else enjoying them. Present a variety of foods at each meal, and be sure to include at least one or two things you know your toddler will eat. Offer him some of everything, but try not to react when he refuses. When my kids were little, they were all picky. One liked starches; another liked proteins, such as chicken and burgers; and the third liked fruits and veggies. So, I always served a dinner with all the components. I usually had some chicken nuggets cooked and waiting or made a PB and J in case nothing else worked. I indulged special orders, such as no sauce or peas but no carrots. As we ate, my husband and I raved about our meal. After a while, the children began to ask for tastes, and before we knew it they became great eaters.

Christine Hierlmaier Nelson

Offer him food. If he won't eat it, then he will be very hungry soon and more willing to eat it later. It usually only takes a day or two before the child realizes that the food on the plate is what's for dinner. If you have been making special meals for him up to this point, it may take longer for him to understand that the practice has changed. Try to explain that big boys or girls eat like this now, if you really want to stop making special meals. He won't starve, especially if you are offering water and juice with the meal and snacks at other times, but he will learn a new routine of eating with the family.

Q I have been trying to get my three-year-old daughter to eat what we are serving for dinner rather than make special meals for her. With much coaxing, she will usually try what we are having, but she then gags and spits it out. I tell her that this is our meal, and she usually goes to bed without eating much. In the morning, she is starving and begging for breakfast. I do try to serve at least one thing she likes at each meal and fit in things she likes throughout the week, such as spaghetti or sloppy joes, but how can I get her to broaden her food horizons so we can have a wider menu?

Pamela Waterman

First, you are doing all the right things—take heart! Some children will carry on like this for years, and parenting does require compromise. Children will not starve themselves, and they do change. Next year, she may start to like a food that she spit out last week. The fact that there is always one thing that she likes is a great happy medium. You can also "beef up" her breakfasts, trying different items that will fill her up then, instead of at night. As long as her doctor says she is doing well, she'll be fine. You may also be surprised when, one day, she asks for what is on your own plate, out of curiosity! For fun, try reading her the wonderful book *Gregory the Terrible Eater* by Mitchell Sharmat.

Penny Warner

Children at this age are very sensitive to the tastes and textures of foods. You can keep offering her a variety of foods to try, but it may take time before she likes anything new. In the meantime, offer her larger portions of her favorite foods, small portions of the new foods you want her to try, and frequent snacks throughout the day. Children have small appetites (and small tummies) but get hungry more frequently due to their high energy levels. As she grows and develops, she'll begin to join you in your meals, but for now, be flexible and continue to offer her the foods she likes, perhaps with other foods, such as veggies, mixed in surreptitiously.

Trish Booth

Family dinners have two parts: the food and the enjoyable experience of eating together. When you put too much emphasis on eating what is served, the pleasure of being together suffers. Children can create an exhausting, emotional scene if you focus only on eating the food served. Most children go through phases of picky eating. When that happens, it is easy to worry about how much your child eats. However, it is not helpful to limit family dinner to only those foods your daughter likes. Accommodate her preferences by having one food item she likes at each dinner. Spaghetti and sloppy joes have a tomato-based sauce in common. Try serving other dishes that have a similar sauce. You can also make main dishes that have other kinds of sauces. When you serve sauceless main dishes, offer her a dip, such as plain yogurt, ranch dressing, ketchup, salsa, or anything else she likes. Keep serving a new food as often as you and other family members want to have it. Serve your daughter a small bit of it and encourage—but don't force—her to eat it. Because she is hungry at breakfast, try using that time to introduce new flavors and textures. Often having a child help prepare part of the meal makes the meal more palatable. Try that approach when you have the energy and patience to let her help. As long as you serve healthy foods, your daughter will be eating healthy foods. She won't starve herself. If you want, add a daily multiple vitamin for that reassurance.

Beverly Willett

I know you're frustrated, but it actually sounds like you're handling everything well. (I'm assuming you've checked with your pediatrician and your daughter is healthy and actually getting enough to eat.) Children develop and broaden their tastes when they're ready. Continue gently encouraging her and gradually testing and adding in new foods. This phase won't last forever. My youngest daughter used to be the original chicken-nuggets or peanut-butter-and-jelly-sandwiches girl. You should see the amazing cook she is today!

Q How do I address the issue and importance of nutrition to my son and daughter-in-law without appearing meddlesome? When our grandson is with us, he seems to eat all the time, so I'm not even sure that is the problem. He is sixteen months old and is still wearing clothing that fits nine-month-olds. His parents are slightly below average in size themselves. In the last four months, our grandson has grown one inch and has gained one pound. The doctor said she won't be very concerned unless she doesn't see a growth spurt by his second birthday. I'm not sure they should wait that long to see if there is a problem. Other than his size, he is developing well—walking, speech, coordination, and so on. Should we be concerned?

Michelle Maidenberg

First, if you are concerned, then you are concerned. As grandparents, it is okay to express concerns as long as it is done respectfully and mindfully. What you need to assess is how open your son and daughter-in-law are to you expressing your concerns. How have they reacted to it in the past? What would be the best way to communicate so that they are able to effectively hear you? If you bring it up, what support can you offer them?

Once you have established all of that, try starting the conversation with what they are doing right and how wonderfully they are raising your grandson. When you speak about what is concerning you, use an *I* statement such as, "I am concerned about him because he hasn't grown all that much lately." Tell them that according to the growth chart you've looked at, you are aware that he is progressing slowly. Ask, "Is that an accurate evaluation I'm making, or is it possible that I'm seeing it all wrong?" Offer to go to the bookstore with them to buy books on infant nutrition, to give them magazine clippings when you find anything pertinent and interesting, or to attend pediatrician appointments if they would like to have you there.

Janet Whalley

Your grandson's growth is slower than most toddlers, but that does not necessarily mean that there is a problem. The most reassuring comment you mentioned was from the doctor. She is aware of the problem and will be following up at his later visits. If you remain concerned, you could ask your son to talk to the doctor at the next visit and ask about what would be done if the growth problem remains at age two.

Then, if he wishes, he could ask if they should do something sooner. The fact that your grandson is developing normally in other domains is reassuring. As children mature they grow in several different domains—physical, mental, social, small-muscle coordination, and large-muscle coordination. It seems that when a child is growing in one domain, the others often lag behind. That could be the case for your grandson. Or he may always be smaller than his peers.

It sounds like your son and daughter-in-law have told you about talking with the doctor, so they may have some concerns, too. I would talk to them about what they are doing to promote their son's growth. Though the growth delay might not be related to your grandson's diet, you could ask if they are giving him any special foods and try to offer those at your home, too. It's okay to tell your son about his eating patterns as a little boy and how you tried to offer a variety of good foods. Then you can talk about what you think are the best foods. Avoid telling them what to do, just tell them about your experiences. Keep the lines of communication open so they will talk to you about your grandson's next health report.

If your son and daughter-in-law are reading a book or an Internet site about feeding toddlers, ask to read it, too. It's helpful to learn about common eating patterns for toddlers. A few characteristics come to mind: Toddlers like to snack more than they like to sit down for a big meal. Because they are working on fine-motor skills, toddlers love finger foods. They may show certain food preferences, but they benefit from having a variety of foods at different times of the day. A good diet for toddlers is like a good diet for older children and adults and includes a variety of vegetables and fruits. Many toddlers like their vegetables slightly steamed rather than raw. To provide whole grains, toddlers love having a small bowl of their favorite dry cereal—though it needs to be a nutritious one. Toddlers often like cheese sticks, easily chewed bites of meat, and plenty of milk. Being a grandparent is joyful, but like parenting, it can also be challenging. Best wishes.

Charlotte Cowan

One of the gold standards in pediatric care is that height and weight (and head circumference until about age three) is measured at every well visit. What matters most is the child's growth along his own growth curve. I would not wait until a child is two years old to assess whether a problem might be present. It will be interesting and important to see what your grandson's weight and height are at his eighteen-month well visit. If he is falling off his growth curve, then it would be appropriate to ask why.

Another more subtle question is how much you can suggest to the parents of your grandchildren without being obtrusive or threatening your relationship. Every family is different. I suspect that it would be smart to air your concerns once. Suggest that your grandchild's growth be brought to the attention of the pediatrician, and leave it at that. Your child will come back to you for advice when and if he wants to.

Eleanor Taylor

As a grandparent, it is natural for you to be concerned about your grandson and to want the best for your family. However, the parents seem to be seeking the advice of a doctor, who is monitoring all aspects of your grandson's growth and development. While your grandson is small, it sounds like his doctor is not worried about his size at this time, especially since the parents are both below average in size. As for what your grandson is eating, children go through times when growth is not rapid, and they often eat less during those periods. Toddlers love to graze throughout the day and eat with their fingers, which is one way they naturally eat the amount of food they need. Periods of food rejection are also normal. One subtle way to help parents is through gifts of books about developmental norms, including eating behaviors and nutritional needs. If you do this in the spirit of helping—not criticizing—your grown children will appreciate your generosity, and you will keep the lines of supportive communication open. Moreover, take the time to read the books yourself so you can feel relaxed and reassured.

Q How do I keep my toddler from eating junk food at other people's houses?

Ashley Hammond

It is perfectly acceptable to discuss your child's diet with people who look after your child. If your son had a food allergy, you would not think twice about it, and the other people would certainly respect your wishes in this regard. The conversation with the parents at the other house, however, will need to be done sensitively. You could write a note and describe typical food choices for your child, giving them "food for thought"!

Pamela Waterman

It's good that you're aware of what your toddler may be eating elsewhere—lots of parents don't seem to care! I assume you're there with your child, so you have several options to try:

- If the timing is right, be sure that your child eats a healthy lunch or snack before heading over to the playdate, so she is less inclined to be hungry and want to fill up on the junk food.
- Bring along your own snacks for her, including some to share with the other children who may be there. Those children may be intrigued by what you brought and may not want the junk food.

- Let your child try a bit of the foods offered, but only after she eats what you brought.
- As others start to eat, take her to another room or bring a special toy for her to play with while she eats what you brought—distraction is always a terrific method!

As she gets older, you might make the compromise that she can only eat junk food as a special treat at someone else's house, but that you don't serve it at yours.

Ilyse Gorbunoff

I don't think you can totally eliminate the allure of junk food. In fact, by making it taboo, your child will be even more inclined to want it. When visiting others, be sure your child has eaten a healthy meal or snack before going, so she will be less hungry and inclined to eat too much. Tell her before you go, "We are going to be guests in someone's home, and some people don't eat the same way we do. It's okay to say, 'No, thank you,' but please be polite. If you would like to have a treat when we are there, you may choose one thing." If you are staying for the visit, you may have some control, but if you are not, it becomes more difficult. Try bringing along your child's favorite healthy treats to share with your hosts. Maybe you can inspire some healthy choices.

Q My first grader won't go to sleep at a decent hour, and my child's teacher says he's always tired at school. What should I do?

Jill Wodnick

Parenting to sleep—not asking a child to put himself to sleep—is an art and science and is really important for the family's overall functioning. Set clear boundaries on bedtime rituals. Spend time snuggling in his bed, playing a guided-relaxation children's CD or nature-sounds CD, or rubbing his feet to add ritual and warmth to the bedtime routine. Singing songs or telling stories can be an important bond for a child's emotional security. Take fifteen or twenty minutes to guide your child to sleep. Focus on gentle touch and making sleep a safe, nurturing time.

Ilyse Gorbunoff

As a teacher, I can tell you how important it is for a child to be well rested for school. As a parent, I understand that this is often easier said than done. Children at this age need about ten hours of sleep; without it they are less able to cope with the rigors of the modern school day. The most important thing is routine. Start by waking your child up early each morning, even the weekends. He'll be more tired at first, but eventually it will work to your advantage. Don't let him nap after school. Be cognizant of the amount of sugar or caffeine he may be having during the day. It's hidden everywhere! Unplug about an hour before bedtime each night—no TV or Internet. Set a timer thirty minutes before the bedtime routine begins so your child understands that bedtime is coming. Establish a routine: a warm bath, one or two stories, and then bed. Sit with your child for a few minutes of cuddle time and quiet talk. Then, off to sleep. Try a reward sticker chart: For each week your child receives five to seven stickers, have a small celebration—a special breakfast, a trip to the playground, and so on. Just don't promise more than you can handle or the whole thing becomes meaningless. It is hard work to establish these bedtime routines, but it will be worthwhile for both of you. I hope you both have sweet dreams from now on!

Vicki Panaccione

Your use of the word *won't* rather than *can't* suggests this is a behavioral issue. If, in fact, he refuses to go to his room or stay in his room, then you will need to take disciplinary action. For instance, you might want to reward him for getting into bed on time, for staying in his bed, for falling asleep by a certain time, and so forth. Or, you may want to put him to bed earlier the next night if his bedtime was too late the previous night.

If he won't go to sleep, what's he doing? You can't actually make him fall asleep, but you can make sure he is not playing with toys, watching TV, or being on the computer. Take any stimulating items out of his room so that he is not playing or reading.

Take a look at your nighttime routine. Children need some wind-down time and a routine that is predictable and leads to lights out. Make sure your son isn't engaged in exciting activities until right before bed; that can keep him up for a while. Instead, close down all electronics an hour before bedtime and have him take a warm bath, spend time reading or listening to music, and just begin to calm down. This should help put him in a more relaxed state for falling asleep. If he still has problems with sleep, contact your pediatrician.

> **Q** My son is two years old. He's never been afraid of the dark, but today he got scared all of a sudden after seeing his shadow in a dim room. He couldn't stop crying out that there were monsters. His behavior and cries of "Monsters, mommy, monsters!" kept on throughout our bedtime routine. Can you offer advice on how to handle this?

Brenda Nixon

All children go through a phase where they are afraid of monsters or spiders or loud noises or going down the drain. It's important for you to remain calm and try to soothe him without making too much of a fuss about it. If he senses you're annoyed or impatient with him, it could make it worse. On the other hand, don't try to reason with a two-year-old and point out that his fears are invalid; to him the fears are very real. *Children's Fears* by Dr. Benjamin Wolman may help. You might find this book—or a similar one—at your local library.

Pamela Waterman

Your son is advanced for two years old! This behavior usually comes a little later—he must be a thinker! Here are several things to try: During the daytime, show him under the bed—let him use a flashlight; perhaps, even move the bed for him and let him see everything during the day. You can also try reading to him from a book such as *There's a Monster in My Closet* by Petra Craddock. Let him make his own shadows. My sister and I loved making our own stuffed-animal shadows dance when we lay in bed at night. Give him a flashlight (you might start during the day), let him line up several small stuffed animals, and have him shine the light to make the shadows. Show him that if he moves the light, the shadows move, too. Let him be in control of making them go sideways or up and down or making them small or large as he moves the flashlight in and out. You can also let him shine it on you while you move, so he sees that mommies or daddies have nice shadows. Use the flashlight to make his shadow. Maybe you can put music on and have him dance and see his shadow dance. If he does not already have one, consider getting him a night-light. There are also flashlights that shut off automatically if he wants to play with one in bed for a while. And realize he may need to come to you in the night, once in a while, for comfort.

Trish Booth

During periods when children make big strides toward independence, they are likely to have moments of upset that show their dependence. It's common for "monsters" and "ghosts" to show up, especially at night. Your response should be a balance between meeting his immediate need for extra assurance and avoiding long-term changes in his bedtime routine. There is no point in offering rational explanations that monsters do not exist, saying that it is just his shadow, or showing him how shadows are made. Acknowledge your son's reaction by saying, "I see you are very upset." Offer to hold him. While you are providing reassurance, firmly tell the monsters to leave. Then, calmly report that you don't see them anymore. If he still does, turn on a light to change the shadow pattern. Another time you may have to rearrange the items that are casting the shadow. Reassure him, again, that the monsters have gone and turn off the light. Then, have a toy stand guard through the night. This should be an important toy, but not his favorite or his lovey. Explain that Mr. Bear will stand guard and keep the monsters away. Or, say that those monsters are afraid of red trucks and will stay away. Try to resume his normal bedtime routine so that he can have the reassurance of that familiarity. If the monsters come back for several nights, consider adding a night-light if he doesn't already have one. Go through the monster-expulsion routine when he raises the issue, but don't start the ritual as a preventative.

Christine Hierlmaier Nelson

Children have huge imaginations about both good and bad things. To him, the monsters are very real; give him just as much real assurance that he is safe. One way to support this is to give him a song, item, or phrase that is specially powered to make the monsters go away. Perhaps purchase a night-light for him when he is not with you. Take it out of the package, and wrap it for him to open like a present; tell him that you got it especially to scare away the monsters: "They don't like this light, and they won't come in your room ever, unless you say it's okay." Try the light out, and if he is still frightened and unsure, tell him that he needs to say the magic words, too: "Monsters be gone!" or "Monsters out!" This will empower him to conquer the monsters in his mind. If you are a religious or spiritual family, you could teach him a special prayer or song to go with the light, such as, "This little light of mine, I'm going to let it shine. No monsters and no baddies, I'm going to let it shine . . ."

Keep in mind that these kinds of fears are normal, and he will outgrow them with your encouragement and love. Tell him he's a strong and brave boy, especially if he uses his light, his song or prayer, and sleeps well again. Teaching him ways to calm himself now will help him later as he faces other fears.

Q How do you get a toddler to sleep in his own bed?

Beverly Willett

I think you have to keep putting him there. My children never had a problem sleeping in their own beds, until our divorce, when my little one started asking if she could sleep with me. We were all going through a rough time, so at first I let her. However, I understood how this could become a crutch, and I began to space it out, letting her sleep with me on weekends. Eventually her discomfort sleeping on her own simply went away. I always made bedtime a ritual and a special occasion—lots of books, stuffed animals to cuddle up with, cozy sheets and blankets, and me singing to my children until they drifted off to sleep. It was exhausting at times, but every moment was well worth it. They adored bedtime, and so did I.

Janet Price

Each family creates its own expectations regarding bedtime, finding the traditions that best reflect the parents' own values and what they each experienced growing up. Were the grandparents strict about bedtimes and where each family member slept? Or did you grow up in a family who took a more easygoing approach to bedtime, letting the child lead? Sometimes we have negative memories of how our bedtimes were handled, and we make a conscious effort to handle this daily ritual differently.

You are not alone with this struggle. Many toddlers enjoy sleeping in their parents' beds, for example, and resist sleeping consistently in their own beds. An important first step is understanding that your child's behavior is communicating something. Since he is so young, he is likely not able to know or tell you what he needs; it is like solving a mystery. Many children feel that their bedrooms are scary—there are shadows at night, which can make familiar items in the bedroom suddenly look strange. Plus, houses often make noises such as creaks or the heater turning on and off. To start, put a night-light in your child's bedroom; leave the bedroom door ajar. A good question to ask yourself is whether he is clear about your expectation for him to sleep in his own bed every night. If you have been feeling ambivalent about this beginning step, it will be hard for you to communicate this expectation clearly. Other potential areas to think about include the possibility that he may have difficulty with transitions or with soothing himself. Provide a consistent bedtime routine, one that is predictable and encourages a winding-down process. This can include bath time, putting on pajamas, brushing teeth, climbing into bed with a favorite stuffed animal or blanket, and snuggling with a parent while listening to a story. A consistent routine helps provide a gradual calming that culminates in the special, brief time in bed listening to the soothing voice of the reader.

Once the child is in bed, with the final steps of the routine completed, say goodnight and leave the room. If the child calls for you, check in one more time. If possible, provide the check-in without re-entering the bedroom. Use as few words as possible, such as, "Goodnight, (name). I love you." Sometimes the child just needs the reassurance of hearing your voice and being reminded that you are still there. Pay attention to what is going on in the home after the child is in bed. Be sure the TV is on low and conversation is quiet and not too close to the toddler's bedroom.

If the toddler is difficult to soothe or has difficulty with transitions, playing a soft recording of sleepy-time music can help. You can find such recordings that have been created specifically for this purpose, or create your own compilation of calming music.

Finally, remember that even after the child is sleeping regularly in his own room, there will probably be times when the child finds himself back in your bed, such as during a thunderstorm. In those moments, gently bring the child back to his own bed, and spend a little time providing reassuring hugs and cuddles. The goal is to ensure that the child does not end up in your bed for the whole night.

Best wishes on this important step of growing independence for your toddler and reclaiming your bed for you!

Tina Nocera

If you speak to other parents, you will find that most have a problem with toddlers staying in their own beds. It was the same in our house. After reading what all the experts had to say, I did something a little different.

The experts suggested that children stay in their own rooms, but I didn't like the message that sent to the children: "Sorry, can't help you now. We're off duty." But at the same time, I really did need a good night's sleep. The compromise was that if the child wanted to come in our bedroom, she could. But she couldn't come in our bed because that was uncomfortable. This worked well for us because the subliminal message was that we were there for our children all the time. Now that our children are adults, we have very good relationships with them.

Q I have a bright and beautiful four-year-old daughter. She is very shy and cautious about everything she does. She is apprehensive about trying new things, and she does everything at a very slow pace. This is very frustrating, and my husband loses patience with this. How can I get him to calm down and her to speed up?

Brenda Nixon

It sounds as if your daughter's temperament is withdrawal. When presented with new stimuli, her first response is to be apprehensive. Eventually, I guess, she warms up and tries new things and makes new friends. You can't push her or devalue the way she's made. However, you can gently encourage her by reminding her of her past successes. Saying something such as, "You tried that new food and liked it," may help ease her self-doubt. Explaining this to your husband may help him become less frazzled with her behavior. As for being pokey, most four-year-olds are. Unless this has been her way of doing things since birth, my guess is that her slow pace is a time-limited problem. Just wait until she's a teen!

Steven Kairys

This is an important issue. Every child has a temperamental personality, and your daughter has the cautious, slow-to-warm style. That is how she is, and your husband needs to understand her better and learn to adapt his style to hers.

Sharon Silver

Asking a child to speed up shows her that this is a hot spot for you, a way for her to control things. There are only four things that a child this young can control: eating, sleeping, when and if she goes potty, and how fast or slow she goes. The developmental stage at four produces the unconscious need to find out how much power a child has in her family, and that stage can't be changed. Going slow is her problem; when dad gets mad, he makes it his problem, too. Try having a family meeting, and all of you decide how you want to manage—not change—this. She has to change this herself, not change because dad is making her. Try a variety of approaches; for example, you could try setting the alarm earlier. She could finish getting dressed in the car if she's making the family late. Give her a certain amount of time to eat, and when the timer goes off dinner is gone. If she doesn't get ready for bed by a certain time, she loses a story.

This may seem harsh for a shy one, but you will make slowness her problem and not yours. You and Dad can be supportive, loving, and empathetic as she learns to live with the consequences of her actions. There will most likely be tantrums from this. Change your mind about what the tantrum represents: The tantrum is really telling you that this approach is working. Weather the tantrums, and be supportive as she has them. Teach her that tantrums won't change things; only deciding to move faster will change things. She needs to know that the world won't wait for her if she is too slow: buses leave, school begins, and so on. Each time she has to live with the results of her actions, try saying, "I know you're upset. I would be, too. Would a hug help?" Then, when she calms down, ask her if there is anything she'll do differently next time so she doesn't have to experience this again. This allows her to do what I call Pulling It through the Brain™. She has to think for herself about why this happened and what she can do to fix it. This is true learning because Mom and Dad do not need to be involved or angry.

Christine Hierlmaier Nelson

Your child has a fearful or anxious temperament. It is just how she is wired to respond to new experiences. Imagine her being an accountant someday or a researcher or a surgeon who must perform exacting work with deliberate caution. As parents, embrace her as she is but give her tools to cope with new experiences or a faster pace. For example, talk with her ahead of time about an appointment or play date, so she knows what to expect. Emphasize the fun parts. Give her extra time to get ready for school, bedtime, and chores so it still fits your schedule. It won't work perfectly every time, so talk to her about the differences in how people get things done—some are fast, and some are slow. Make a game called Speedy Go to see if she can beat you to the car or get dressed faster than you. Encourage her when she completes a task faster than normal. And, be ready when she resists experiences like sleepovers, the first day of school, or a day camp. She will need time to adjust to any new surroundings and people, but your encouragement will help her feel secure. Her personality is like her eye color: beautiful and fixed. Your patient teaching and playfulness will get better results.

Q My son, who has just turned five, has still been having potty accidents. I recently made him a chart, and it has been helping, but now his preschool teacher has suggested he might have ADD. Lately, I have been analyzing his every move, and I worry that he does have it. He still acts like a toddler and gets into things. He also does well with puzzles and playing by himself, which I heard is a red flag. I always thought he was just active like my older son, who also doesn't sit still. How do I know if this is just his personality or if I need to have him checked for ADD?

Naomi Drew

Why don't you give him a little more time and give him the benefit of the doubt? It sounds as though he'll be starting kindergarten in the fall. Try to hang in there over the summer, and see how he does when he enters kindergarten.

For now, if you possibly can, let him be a child. Enjoy him, and try putting your worries aside. If you're not able to do that, contact your school district to see if they have any preschool evaluation measures that can be used to give him an initial assessment.

Ellen Gibran-Hesse

In raising my sons, ages twenty-four and twenty-one now, I noticed that most little boys are very active. I think that many teachers are far too quick to pounce on the idea of a child having ADD instead of acknowledging the fact that school is designed for more sedentary activities and personalities.

You have good instincts about helping your son. The fact that you created the chart so your little one can focus on it to help himself says a lot. It's also a good idea to keep him active to run down his energy. Change activities frequently to keep his focus and interest. If your little one enjoys puzzles and alone time, I'd say he is curious and focused enough for his age. Don't worry!

Tina Nocera

Moving is a good thing, not a warning signal for ADD. I am concerned that teachers are using this response as a catchall. But the question of your child having ADD is something you should discuss with your pediatrician; she can give you more information.

Please remember that five-year-old boys don't sit still; they're just not wired that way, and it is okay. The potty accidents can be frustrating, but as they say, this too shall pass. Children forget to go because they get caught up in play and don't listen to their bodies.

What you might try is to make going to the bathroom a part of a daily routine. You can even make light of it and introduce the pee-pee dance if he feels the need. Tell him you will watch for the dance and remind him to go, but let him know that he is in control and needs to learn to go on his own.

I'm not of fan of embarrassing a child nor rewarding a child for going to the bathroom. If you are consistent with an approach, establish a routine, and help him to be aware of and listen to his body, this problem will correct itself.

Q My daughter is four years old and has no desire to be potty trained. I've tried taking away her toys, bribing her with things she wants, making her sit on the potty for long periods of time, and so on. I've been working on this for almost two years! I don't know what else to do.

She does pretty well with pee-peeing in the potty but has yet to poo-poo in the potty. Also, she tries to hold her bowel movements, which just ends up making her constipated. I'm at my wits' end. I'd like to think that she will just do it when she is ready, but I'm beginning to wonder.

Steven Kairys

It would be good to see a pediatric gastroenterologist. She appears to be stool-holding and then, when she finally defecates, it becomes even more uncomfortable and sometimes painful. For this situation, a doctor can give some sort of laxative that is titrated so the stool is soft but not runny. The child will not be able to hold back, and then the toilet training can really begin.

Brenda Nixon

Back off, Mom. Your four-year-old daughter is literally resisting your pressure to perform. If you ease up and act like you don't care, then she'll regain control over herself and use the toilet. There is no reason to work on toileting for two years. If a child is ready, has parents who can commit the time and energy to the task, and is given encouragement (never punishment), then she will be motivated to use the potty.

Of course she's constipated—this is called anal retention. She is learning to stubbornly control the situation, even if she has to retain her stool. This is physically and emotionally unhealthy. Beginning today, simply say to her, "You're a big girl now. You can put your pee-pee and poo-poo in the potty. If you don't, then you'll have to clean up yourself."

Try to be calm and matter-of-fact about it. In life, when you make a mess, don't you have to clean it up yourself? Then, so should your daughter. When your four-year-old messes herself, calmly announce to her that she must go to the bathroom and clean herself up. By taking ownership of her mess, she'll be more invested in using the toilet for good. Best wishes from a mom of two daughters.

Trish Booth

Children and parents can pretty easily get into tugs of war over potty training. Unfortunately, children have the advantage. Daytime bladder training usually comes before bowel training. Because your daughter is able to control her bladder, the issue is not likely to be a physical problem. It is most likely a battle of wills.

I suggest dropping the issue for a month to let things cool down. Use pull-up diapers that allow her to use a potty if she wants and allow easier clean-up when she doesn't. It will be very hard, but say nothing about toilet behavior. This means no praising when she uses the potty and no statements of disappointment or disgust when she doesn't.

After things have cooled down and you feel it's no longer a big issue between you, set a date for "P Day" (the day she starts wearing real panties or underwear) that is two weeks away. Make it a day on which you have nothing else planned. Make a big deal of this! Put it on your activity calendar, and each day announce how many days until P Day. Two days before P Day, take her shopping to pick out her underwear. Buy whatever design she likes. Do this even if she already has "big-girl" underwear. Then, the morning of P Day, box up her pull-ups and give her a pair of her new panties to wear. Cheerfully tell her that is what she is wearing from now on because she is a big girl. Big girls wear panties because big girls use the potty.

For the next few days, there will be a lot of accidents of both kinds. And this is the hardest part—with every accident you will need to stay matter-of-fact and positive when you tell her to clean herself up and put on dry clothes. She may need help with cleaning after bowel accidents, but leave as much of the cleanup as possible to her. You can suggest she use the potty a few times in the day, saying, "It's almost time. Do you want to use the potty before you start?" But, don't hound her or set consequences if she doesn't.

After she discovers that she isn't pushing your buttons by not complying, she will start paying attention to her own comfort. The number of accidents will decrease. When she does finally poo-poo on the potty, tell her warmly that you are proud of her and you knew she could do it. Praise her but don't make a huge deal of it. Expect the process to take a month or six weeks before the accidents are rare. You'll see improvement week to week.

Most parents use diapers or pull-ups for nighttime until children have a good track record of not having accidents. Because nighttime dryness is more complicated than daytime, you may want to use pull-ups for a while. Although the nighttime transition takes longer, there usually isn't the same battle of wills.

Pamela Waterman

First, pat yourself on the back for patience; with some children, that's simply what it takes. All three of my daughters were more than four years old before the concept finally seemed to sink in! They just didn't care. And one of them still wet her bed until age seven, at which time we had the doctor give us a prescription for a nasal spray that did the trick. I'm assuming you've spoken to your doctor to make sure your child is in good health.

I'd back off on your efforts in the bathroom. Try going a month without making any big deal about it, and then revisit the topic. Just make sure she is getting lots of water and some juice and applesauce. Start talking (casually) about different activities that she'll be allowed to do when she's potty trained and can wear big-girl panties, such as gymnastics or swimming in the big pool. Let her pick out her own packages of underwear to have in the drawer for when it's time.

We found that our children would get so involved in what they were doing they didn't want to leave it to go potty, even when they knew they needed to. You could bring the toy or book into the bathroom if you realize that she needs to go. Does she have any friends who are already potty trained? Will she head to kindergarten in the fall? You don't want to do verbal comparisons, since everyone is different, but I wonder if over the summer the thought of kindergarten amongst the friends will be an incentive. If she's not frustrated, just indifferent, I'd wait and ride it out.

Q My four-and-a-half-year-old son has been having potty accidents for more than a year. He poops in his pants and is constantly soiling himself. It's become very upsetting and frustrating. I have tried reward systems and reminding him to go. It also happens in preschool during the day, but not every day. I am at my wits' end! I always have to bring a change of clothes for fear it will happen all the time. He doesn't seem embarrassed at all by this. Please let me know what else I can do!

Ilyse Gorbunoff

The first thing you must do is speak to your pediatrician about this problem. There could be a physical reason for this. You don't want to have a battle over something your son can't help. That could only make you both feel worse. He may just be constipated and can't go when he needs to. Maybe try more water and fiber in his diet.

After you see the doctor, the next thing is to try a schedule. Do the accidents occur around the same time every day? If, for instance, his accidents occur in the morning, try putting him on the toilet every day after breakfast and encourage him to sit there for ten minutes. You can try this after every meal, if it's feasible. Keep him company. Read a book or sing a song. Use a sticker chart to reward him for sitting the ten minutes. (My son loved toy catalogs in which we circled the things he could get when his sticker chart was complete.) Make a big deal when he poops in the potty. Maybe two stickers for success! Instead of rewarding each day without an accident, which he may not be able to control, you will be rewarding each time for something he can control. You will both feel better.

Steven Kairys

Your son will need to see your pediatrician or pediatric gastroenterologist. He is most likely stool-holding and has a large mass of stool in his colon and rectum. Part of stool-holding is poor colon motion that leads to soiling and losing the sensation of having to go to the bathroom. This is now a medical problem and not a behavioral one. He will need to be cleaned out and then be placed on a regimen to gradually regain control and better function of his intestines.

Brenda Nixon

First, the word *accident* means an occasional, unpredicted event. If your four-and-a-half-year-old is constantly doing something for more than a year, it's not an accident but a planned, habitual behavior.

Second, be sure to check with your son's pediatrician to ensure there isn't a medical complication making it impossible for him to hold his poop.

Third, bringing a change of clothes is sending him the message that it's okay to soil himself. Stop sending extra clothes. Let him know your expectation: "Keep your clothes clean by putting your poop in the potty."

Fourth, if he soils himself, instruct his teachers to escort him to the bathroom and supervise while he cleans up his own poop. Sure it's disgusting—it is for any adult who has to clean him, too. He made the mess; he can clean it up.

At home, if he soils himself, supervise while he cleans up his own poop. Once your son realizes that he will face the consequence of this undesirable behavior, he'll choose a new behavior: pooping in the potty. Good luck, and stay strong and consistent.

Whining, Complaining, and Blaming

Chapter 2

Q How do you get a four-year-old to stop whining?

Brenda Nixon

Believe it or not, whining is associated with language development. Most children go through a phase of whining—although it's quite unpleasant for us adults. Just because something is developmental doesn't mean you must accept it. You are right to want to put an end to whining, and the best way is to simply make a statement such as, "Speak in your big-boy voice," then mildly turn away to ignore the whining. When your child speaks in a regular, nonwhining voice, you can respond to his need. If your child persists in whining, persist in ignoring until you get the desired tone of voice. Also, remember your power to persuade and model appropriate behavior—be sure you don't whine so you're not modeling this behavior to your child.

Christine Hierlmaier Nelson

Children whine because it works for them—because you respond. Stop responding. Tell your child that you will respond when he is asking in a nice way and using manners. With enough repetition and consistency, your child will get the message that whining will not get him what he wants. Plus, he will learn that it's rude. After all, who wants a child who grows up to be an adult who whines?

Trish Booth

Four-year-olds can seem so grown up at times that their regression to whining can be quite vexing. Here are some suggestions to reduce whining under several circumstances:

Because four-year-olds are aware of the power of their speech, you can address some whining head on. When your child starts to whine because she wants you to do something, cut in and identify her tone of voice as whining. Then, tell her that whining hurts your ears and makes it hard to hear what she is saying. Tell her that she needs to talk in a nicer voice. Whenever the whining starts, calmly remind her that you can't understand her because she is whining. As soon as the tone of her voice improves, let her know you can hear her now that she is talking nicely. Repeat her request in a pleasant voice to reinforce the change, and then deal with the request. Over time and with many reminders of your inability to understand her whining, your child will whine less.

Some whining is driven by the situation, including being hungry, tired, or overwhelmed. It is more effective to deal with these times by changing the situation, if that is possible. Children often whine in the late afternoon after being at preschool or day care. You may be able to head off some whining by having a small, healthy snack available for the ride home or as soon as you get home. If your child is at home with you in the afternoon, consider having a thirty-minute quiet time after lunch or later in the day. Set a timer and have your child go to her room for this period of quiet play. Let her play with toys, color, or "read" books, or let her listen to soft music or a recorded story. Don't turn on the TV or start a video or DVD; these options don't give her an opportunity to control her environment and rest. This gives your child a break in the action and time to regroup. If she is really tired, she may fall asleep. Pitch this as a positive part of the day, not like a time-out.

If whining occurs because your child does not want to leave an activity or go to a necessary one, it is best to ignore the whining. Instead, simply and clearly state what needs to be done, and give your child a task: "It's time to go now. Here is your jacket. Please put it on." Stay focused on each task that needs to be done to reach your destination, and praise her for her cooperation.

Jill Wodnick

Your child needs verbal modeling for redirection. In a calm, clear voice you can say, "Please ask for the milk politely, like this," and then model the tempo and tone you would like for her to use. Working on tone and tempo through modeling sentences and phrases is important. Using repetitive phrases works well for four- and five-year-olds, so she can be directed to say, "I notice that..." as a way of describing the place and physicality of an event. The website www.responsiveclassroom.org has many phrases that are useful not just for classrooms but also for homes to help children of all ages learn to communicate in a culture of respect and empowerment.

Vicki Panaccione

It sounds as though your child is regressing. She was talking in a pre-K voice, and now she's whining. First order of business: Explore why she is whining! Children's behavior is almost always telling us something if we stop to figure it out, rather than simply trying to do away with it. Many children regress in response to some kind of change, trauma, or occurrence in their lives. Is there conflict or change in the family? Are the demands of school too much for her? Is she being mistreated in some way? Her behavior may be a barometer for something amiss in her life. You may want to talk with your pediatrician or find a child psychologist to evaluate what's going on.

The key to whining is not to give in to it. Giving in to whining only teaches kids to whine. Instead, encourage her to use her big-girl voice, and let her know that you will be happy to accommodate her when she does.

Ellen Gibran-Hesse

Your child has learned this is the way to get attention, a response, or what she wants. The good news is that she learned it, so she can unlearn it, too. I would bet she responds well to a star system, a positive reward system for new behavior. Put up a large poster board with the days of the week written on it. Be very clear about what whining is, and tell her that you want her to learn how not to whine. Initially, she will get a warning that she is whining, and you can give her an example of how to rephrase. If she does, she gets a star. At the end of the week, if she has achieved a certain number of stars, she will get a defined reward. Make sure it is a reward she will want to work toward, and keep it simple.

If she whines after a warning, she loses a star. End the system once she goes to kindergarten–she should be done by then anyway. You may want to share this approach with her pre-K teacher. She can either create her own star system or report to you with a maximum number of stars for the day to put on your board.

Ilyse Gorbunoff

I think I would start by telling your child that she is almost ready for kindergarten. Tell her all about kindergarten and how much fun she will have, but stress that only big boys and girls can go. Tell her that, in kindergarten, no whining is allowed, so from now on you're going to start practicing. Together, come up with a code word that you will use if you hear whining. This will help her save face, and it kind of makes it fun. Pick something funny. At my house, we used *flounder*. When my son whined, I would ask, "Do you smell flounder?" It became such a funny thing that he would often laugh and forget why he was whining in the first place. Your child may not know what whining means. By highlighting it this way, she'll be able to identify the behavior. When she whines, say the code word as a reminder, and then model how she should say the same thing without whining. It will take some time, but she'll get it after a while.

Q I have a bright, five-year-old girl and a boy who is two and a half. I always find myself yelling when I'm with my daughter. She's always complaining and blaming others for any problems or mistakes. Is it really possible to calm down when my kids are driving me nuts?

Steven Kairys

Try to talk less and act more. Understand why your daughter complains so much, but don't respond to the complaints at the moment. Give her attention for being positive, and ignore the negative times. When the reasons for her complaints are clear, try to find some solutions that work. Give her some choices that you are comfortable with.

Vicki Panaccione

Yes, absolutely. And here's a question for you: What are you doing for you? Is your daughter always on your last nerve? My guess is that you are not taking care of yourself, a very common problem among mothers of young children. If you don't take time to recharge your batteries, then there's nothing left when it comes time to deal with the annoyances that a five-year-old is bound to exhibit. Yelling tends to be a signal that moms are on overload. You probably bypass all those good parenting ideas quickly. So, first suggestion: Take time for you. It could be as simple as a soak in a bubble bath or signing up for a yoga or pottery class. You might call a friend or go out to lunch. What makes your heart sing? Add it into your life.

Second piece of advice: You yell in frustration, and she whines and complains for the same reason! Is whining and complaining a new behavior? If so, what might be going on with your child? Is she tired, stressed, or hungry by the time you see her? Or does she lack frustration tolerance? Children at this age become accomplishment oriented and develop the need to succeed. So, she may be having a difficult time from a developmental standpoint. Why is she complaining? Perhaps she needs you to teach her problem-solving skills, good decision making, or how to be a good sport.

Take a deep breath before dealing with her. Your calm demeanor will not only help you help her more effectively, but it will also serve as a model for how she can deal with her own frustrations.

Michelle Maidenberg

First, it is important to acknowledge that just because you are yelling doesn't mean you're "losing it" or you are a bad mother, even though it may feel this way. These are all very normal feelings and ones that most of us mothers unfortunately share.

You mentioned yelling at your daughter and then followed it up by saying that she is always complaining or blaming others. There is something about her behaviors and reactions that is pushing certain buttons in you. I recommend that you understand why these behaviors induce these feelings in you. Having insight into this will allow you to gain perspective into your reaction to her and will help you become more conscious of when these feelings are getting induced. You may also be able to predict when they will be induced. The goal is that you will inevitably be better able to control your acting-out behavior.

It is absolutely possible and essential for you to calm down. Modeling is critical. In general, if we want our children to be controlled and behave in ways that we consider socially appropriate, we need to model these behaviors. This takes much effort, patience, and care. It is obvious by your question that you really want to change and care immensely about your children. You can change! There are wonderful books that I highly recommend that will help you to reduce yelling and increase understanding with your little ones: *1, 2, 3 Magic: Effective Discipline for Children 2–12 by Thomas W. Phelan and How To Talk So Kids Will Listen and Listen So Kids Will Talk* by Adele Faber and Elaine Mazlish. They will most definitely help you with your journey. Best of luck!

Q I have a five-and-a-half-year-old daughter. She is very sulky all the time and tends to look at the negative side of things. It really drives me crazy, but most important, it seems to affect her trying new things or improving at things she knows. Her first reaction to new things is no. And when things don't go her way, her first reaction is anger. How can I encourage her to react to things in a more productive manner?

Brenda Bercun

There are many children who are insecure about trying new things or who do not want to work at improving what they can do. These children may also have trouble with transitions from one activity to another. Is this a new behavior or has it been part of her personality all along? If this is a relatively new behavior, is there anything that has happened to produce this change? Has there been a change or a loss in the family or a move to a new home or school? If the answer is yes, then this behavior may be part of an adjustment issue and should be addressed. I would encourage you to talk with your daughter at a time when the two of you are spending some alone time. In a gentle, nonjudgmental manner, bring up your observation of her resistance, and ask her if she knows why she doesn't like doing new things. Ask her what worries her about it or what she doesn't like about it. If she starts to talk, just listen and understand her feelings. If she says she doesn't know, ask her to think about it because understanding her reasoning is very important. Let her know that her ability to be happy and successful is very important and that understanding what makes her unhappy will help to work it out.

When your child is upset, encourage her to talk about what is upsetting her. Help her develop the language of self-expression in an appropriate manner. Teach her the meaning of being angry, sad, disappointed, or frustrated. Encourage her to express those feelings. Teach her how to manage these emotions by discussing these scenarios at a calm time, and help her understand what she can do when she is feeling them. Sometimes she may need to give herself a positive time-out to calm down and figure out how to problem solve. You can help by asking her what she can do about this. What does she think? How can she make the situation better? If she can't come up with answers, ask if you can help problem solve with her. Come up with a few suggestions, and talk about whether they will work. Support her efforts to figure things out with positive feedback and lots of hugs. This process takes time, but it will be well worth it. Life is full of challenges, and figuring out how to navigate them is an essential skill.

I encourage you to pay attention to how you model problem solving to your daughter. Let her know how you have handled difficult situations that are appropriate for her to hear. Talk to her about when you tried a new activity and you didn't know anyone or you were uncomfortable because you didn't know how to do something and how you managed it. Or talk about a time when you didn't get what you wanted. Talk about being sad, upset, disappointed, or frustrated. Model your use of language to express being upset. I would also talk to her about your daily successes, and ask her about hers. Good things that happen are successes as well as successful problem solving. Put a lot more energy into the successes so that you can each experience the power of that. In our daily lives there are many more successes than not. Often, it is just a matter of where we shine the light. Reinforce her efforts toward change with positive feedback. Children thrive on being seen for their efforts and accomplishments.

Jim Taylor

Your daughter's reactions are consistent with a fear of failure. Are you or your husband perfectionists? Do you focus on results and show disappointment (perhaps without any awareness on your part) when she fails to live up to your expectations? The fact that "it really drives you crazy" suggests this might be the case. Look in the mirror and make sure your messages are about the three Ps: positive, process, and progress. As for your daughter's anger, that emotion is never the real emotion but is a defensive emotion that protects her from a much more painful deeper emotion, usually fear. Ask yourself what she is afraid of (usually failure and the loss of her parents' love). The bottom line is that your daughter is avoiding something that she perceives as too threatening to face. You need to figure out what that fear is and how you can remove the fear. If you're unable to figure it out on your own, professional guidance might be helpful.

Beverly Willett

Sorry to hear you're having trouble. The first thing I'd suggest is speaking with her teacher, caregiver, or anyone else she spends substantial time with to determine if there's something bothering her. In general, children often mirror those around them, so it's important to think about whether the people around her tend to be negative as well. Try to keep a positive frame of mind yourself, and point out the positive things you notice around you and about her.

It's also important not to minimize her feelings if she's feeling upset. Try to honor those feelings and at the same time help her turn them around. If she's using anger to get her way, try to make sure you're not giving in to that so she'll learn that anger is never an effective strategy.

Even at her age, I don't think she's too old for time-outs. When I started meditating several years ago, it struck me how meditating is something akin to a time-out for adults—time to take a deep breath and create space in our world between the frustrations we might be feeling and the solutions that are out there that we just can't see. If you can gently divert your daughter's attention when she's angry and construct some sort of modified time-out, help her create space and then come back to the problem. Then, talk to her about solutions. It will take a great deal of patience on your part, but ultimately one of our jobs as parents is to help our children develop ways of finding solutions. The problems and frustrations of daily life will never end. Hopefully, when your daughter learns to see that she is capable of finding solutions, she'll be able to move off her anger more quickly. Don't forget to compliment her, too, when she's able to figure things out on her own.

As for trying new things, I'd suggest making sure you honor her feelings. For her to gain confidence, it's important to start small. Think of things she can attempt and succeed at so that she can become familiar with succeeding and start building confidence, little by little. And don't forget to tell her what a good job she did.

Ashley Hammond

Children thrive on positive reinforcement and success, at any task. Choosing tasks and activities that are easily broken down and that have an opportunity for success at an early stage will be ideal for her. Failure is also an important part of growth. Children express their frustration with failure in many ways, as do adults. Parents and family members modeling good behavior in similar situations at home is crucial, as this is another domain where children learn. Take small steps; allow for success and failure without overreacting to either; and model good behavior.

Friend Issues, Bullies, and Peer Pressure

Q During playtime, our two-year-old lets other kids bully her. If she is on a swing and another child tries to shove her off, she will immediately get down and let the other child sit. How can we teach her to stand up for herself?

Jill Wodnick

Two-year-olds are still preverbal in many of the complex sentence structures that older children use on the playground. Playgrounds are wonderful places for toddlers to run and jump, but it will really be up to you or your partner or caregiver to help honor her needs. If you hear an older child trying to push her off, simply stand up for her and explain she is two years old and will be on the swing for another few minutes.

Being a leader by example is how you teach your daughter to advocate for and give voice to her own needs. At her age, she is still very connected with you and needs your phrases, sentences, and leadership so her time on playgrounds is meaningful and safe.

Tina Nocera

It's a challenge when we see our children being taken advantage of. Likely, we think back to our own experiences and always hope for better for our children. But, at her age, I wouldn't be too worried about it.

Somewhere between ages two and three and a half, she will start to react to other children pushing her out of the way or taking her toys. It's a good idea to protect her at this point and stand up for her. Tell the other child, "Right now, it's (child's name)'s turn, and next it will be your turn." She will internalize and learn from your assertiveness. When she does start to react to others, it's important to talk to her about how she feels. Help her name her feelings by asking, "Did that make you sad or angry when that happened?" It's a good idea to name feelings early.

You can also give her some good things to say when someone takes her toys or pushes her out of the way. If you start to notice this becoming a real problem as she moves into being ages three and four and she is not reacting to others' aggression, then I would start reflecting to her, "This is how I would feel if that had happened to me."

Brenda Bercun

It appears that your daughter may need some guidance on how to assert herself in a kind, clear manner. She may not be one who is comfortable with confrontation, and at her age she may not have the language skills or the social skills to communicate her desires.

The playground is a fabulous arena for teaching cooperation, patience, and manners among a community of children.

The next time you witness this type of behavior from another child toward your daughter, I encourage you to intervene by asking the child who attempted to shove her off the swing if he would like a turn. If the answer is yes, give the child the language to ask for a turn. I would then ask your daughter if she is done and ready to get off the swing. If the answer is yes, support your daughter in getting off the swing and encourage the other child to say thank you. If your daughter is not ready to get off the swing, allow her to swing for another minute or two, letting the other child know that as soon as your daughter is finished, he will have a turn. After a minute or two, encourage your daughter to allow the other child a turn at the swing, letting her know that taking turns is part of playground behavior.

I hope that other parents in your community support the teachings of cooperation and good manners and will be able to create a courteous playing environment.

Q My four-year-old daughter is not being treated fairly at preschool. She says that some of the kids are being mean to her. It is starting to affect her personality. I notice how much she has changed since starting at this school. I want to transfer her to a new school, but there is a waiting list. What do I do in the meantime? Should I keep her home until we find a new school or have her keep attending the present school hoping that things won't get worse? I am very confused as a parent. I want to do the right thing for my daughter, and of course I want to do what makes her happy.

Vicki Panaccione

Good communication between parents and school personnel is very important, no matter what age or grade your child is in. While she ultimately may need to change schools, I would encourage you to try to work with the school initially. Set a good example for your child—try to work out problems rather than just leave the situation.

What do you mean when you say she is being treated unfairly? What is your daughter experiencing to make her or you feel that way? Talk to the teachers about your daughter's unhappiness and reports about the school and her peers. Let them know about the changes you have seen in her personality, and voice your concerns. Find out what they see at school and what, if anything, they have tried to do to make the situation better. If they are not aware of a problem, they may need to provide more supervision or be more mindful when your daughter is in an area of potential conflict.

In the meantime, it wouldn't hurt to put your name on the waiting list for the other school. When your turn comes up, you'll have an option to stay at the school where the problem has hopefully been resolved or change to a new environment. However, if your child continues to remain unhappy and you feel the situation is unworkable, then bring her home until the other program is available.

Charlotte Cowan

There are several important points in your question. You clearly care deeply about helping your daughter. She is very lucky to have you as her mom! Going to school at almost any age can be difficult for every child and her parents. You do not tell me in your question whether your daughter has already had school experience somewhere else or whether this is the first time for her to be in a group of children. Either way, there are lots of adjustments to make. Children need to learn how to share, how to be kind, how to respect differences, how to play with others fairly, and so on. This is a big job for any child.

First, I suggest that you speak with the teachers about your concerns. Teachers know what is going on in the classroom and are often very helpful at identifying problems. Another suggestion is that you volunteer to spend some time at your daughter's school. Can you help with art class, reading, or special holidays? By being present in the classroom, you would get to know firsthand what is going on. Third, help your daughter to make friends in the classroom. To break down her sense that everyone is mean to her, invite one or two children over to play or to meet at a playground. Learning to make her current situation better is a good first step toward helping your daughter enjoy the school years that stretch out ahead of her. Best of luck, and I hope this helps!

Janet Price

It can be excruciating to see your little one unhappy in her school setting. It sounds like you have made up your mind about changing schools. Regarding whether to keep her home until the new placement becomes available: Is she asking to stay home each day and making the transition from home to school difficult? Does she seem to be getting nothing or very little that is positive from her time at school? If the answers to these questions are yes, then she should probably stay home while she waits for a spot in the other school. Deciding when to terminate a difficult placement for your child and when to encourage your child and work with the staff to make school a better experience can be difficult. I have some questions that you might want to ask her teachers, if you haven't yet: Do they notice that your daughter is struggling with peer connections? Are they aware that she feels others are being mean to her? What are they doing to help make that work better for your daughter in their class? Working together in a school-home partnership can do wonders in making school an environment that is positive for her. Best of luck in whatever you decide.

Christine Hierlmaier Nelson

Are you able to take a day off from work and observe the dynamics of the classroom? This may be step one in getting to the bottom of what is occurring. Second, enlist the assistance of the teacher and staff in observing any unfair behavior in the classroom. The children should not be running the show; the teachers should be modeling and teaching appropriate behavior. Your daughter has the right to feel safe and should be able to turn to an adult in the classroom for reassurance.

You can also have conversations with your daughter about how to handle teasing or rude behavior. If children have tools, they can often adapt. For example, if a child is teasing her, she can say, "I know you really like me and that's why you're teasing me. It's okay, I like you, too." She is more likely to believe the loving words of her parent than the teasing words of a classmate. Tell her that children sometimes tease, but what they say isn't true. Tell her that she is beautiful and loving. Build her up at home to handle the adversity that life brings.

Brenda Bercun

It is very distressing to parents when their children are having difficult experiences that are affecting their well-being. Before taking your daughter out of the school, I would encourage you to address your concerns with the teacher and head of the school. Perhaps they could assist your daughter and the other children involved in learning to be kind and inclusive. Perhaps they could teach appropriate language skills to express hurt feelings and promote cooperation.

Is there anything you can do to promote friendships with these children outside of school? Perhaps you can befriend one of the parents and invite them for a play date to a park or your home. The relationship could shift when the environment changes.

If these don't seem like viable options, I encourage you to explore other schools that might be a better fit. In the meantime, evaluate your options. How long would it be before she is accepted into the new school? How many more months are there in the school year? Are there camps that she could attend during the summer months? If you had her home, would you be able to provide a stimulating environment that includes socialization and learning opportunities?

Having your daughter feel emotionally safe in school is essential for her ability to learn and mature. Being able to have friends and learn social skills is a big part of being four years old.

Q My daughter is four years old. She has a friend the same age whom she calls her best friend. My daughter follows this girl around like a puppy. The problem is that the best friend can be bossy. She often talks down to my daughter and will dump her to play with another child. Yesterday she told my daughter, "Allysa and me talked it over, and you can play with us now." Even with this poor treatment, my daughter continue to wants to play almost exclusively with her best friend. How do I teach her that she should not accept treatment like this? Or will she learn this on her own? I want her to develop strong, positive self-esteem.

Charlotte Cowan

There are many issues in your daughter's friendship with and dependence on her "best friend." Children her age are busy learning about friendship, and there is much negotiating back and forth as they learn about sharing, kindness, and inclusion. A good resource for you might well be your daughter's preschool teacher. She will see your daughter in a group situation for many hours a week, and she is in a perfect position to help the groups of girls interact appropriately. The teacher may also have some tricks for you to try at home, such as intervening whenever you hear anything hurtful being said by any child (including your daughter). Try saying something like, "In our house, we have the rule that . . ." Such intervention by a grownup can be very helpful and can teach the children good behavior.

Norman Hoffman

Some children follow the misguided suggestions and lead of particular playmates. Unfortunately, some of the more dominant, uncaring types may influence them into trouble. When uncaring, dominant children influence the less dominant, more caring children, this combination can lead to tragic consequences.

It is essential that you recognize and identify your own child's less dominant characteristics. If you believe your child is easily influenced by her friend's more dominant and "bossy" personality, you must take action. What action you take is highly related to the personality of your child and how she accepts your suggestions. It is important to understand the most effective manner to approach her. Some children, for example, take suggestions well, while others may engage in a power struggle. I suggest that you obtain children's reading material to share with your daughter about bullying, bad influences, and heightening self-esteem and awareness. Your child may feel that she is inferior, or she may have poor or low self-esteem, and she may feel that she must do everything she can to keep her friendship with the other girl.

Address this issue now or your daughter may face dire consequences later in her development.

Trish Booth

It's hard to watch our children be bossed around and treated poorly, because we want the best for them. In addition, the poor treatment can bring back memories of our own childhoods. Although friends are important at four, friends at this age don't have the power they do during the teen years.

How upset does your daughter get when she is bossed around? If your daughter is bothered by the behavior, you have a starting place to talk about more appropriate behavior. That could include suggesting that your daughter use *I* statements to tell her friend how the bossy behavior makes her feel: "I feel sad when you don't let me play with you." Your daughter, however, may not be ready for that kind of confrontation.

If you feel that the friend's behavior is damaging your daughter's self-esteem, the best way to help is to expand your daughter's activities and have play dates with other children. Choose an activity that your daughter likes, and invite another classmate or neighbor to participate. This approach works better than preventing your daughter from seeing her "best friend."

Your daughter's relationship with her bossy friend is likely to change. She may tune in to the bossing and decide she doesn't want to be treated that way. If there are developmental differences that give the other child an advantage, these will likely disappear over time. Your daughter may, on her own, find another best friend. This will likely happen if she develops an interest that isn't shared by her current best friend.

Georgianna Duarte

It sounds like it is time to discuss the meaning of what a friend is. There are numerous books at the library. Talk to your local librarian or a teacher about friendship books, and in the interim discuss the issue with your daughter and create a picture of what a good friend is. Tell her that a good friend is someone who shares, talks nicely, and so on. Let your daughter create the picture, and help guide her to identify the key characteristics of a good friend. Use yourself and your own friends as an example. A "best friend" is an unrealistic idea for a four-year-old, so focus on simply the concept of *friendship* and what that means.

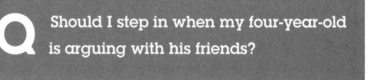

Q Should I step in when my four-year-old is arguing with his friends?

Although it is tempting to step right in, it's important that young children learn to solve their own conflicts. However, sometimes they don't have the tools or even the language to do so. Use the conflict as a teachable moment. You can model the correct behavior and give the children the language they need. I would recommend giving the children a few minutes to work it out. Often, the problem will resolve quickly. If this doesn't happen, it's time to intervene. Speak to the children in a concerned but calm way. What looks like a silly argument to an adult can be very important to a four-year-old. Let each child tell his or her side in order to validate the children's feelings. Say that you understand how each one feels, and ask them to validate the other child's feelings. Explain that friends (or siblings) don't treat each other in this manner and that, when you care about a person, compromising is important. (Of course, you will have to give a four-year-old explanation of *compromise*.) Ask them to tell you how they could resolve the conflict. If they don't have the language to do so, give suggestions and have them repeat them. Ask them to hug, shake hands, or high five. Next, engage them in an activity. Before you know it, they'll be best friends again. Compliment them on how they are getting along. The next time they have a play date, remind them that friends compromise because they care about each other. If you keep repeating the message, they'll get it, and they'll have the tools and motivation to get along.

Mark Borowski

This is difficult to answer without a little more information, but here are some considerations. In my opinion, the arguing is not a concern since disagreements are a natural occurrence between people. This is especially true with children; they are self-centered and not mature enough to discuss and resolve. They often don't have the communication skills to resolve conflicts.

So, the issue is more about how they're arguing. If they are being disrespectful, name calling, or being aggressive, I would step in. If not, I would listen in and see how they're progressing to a resolution. You can either let them resolve the conflict themselves, or you may need to help with the resolution. Get a clear understanding of each child's position and help make a decision or provide some options, then let them decide.

Consider the values you want to teach your children, particularly in the context of playing with friends. For example, whenever our children have had friends over, we have explained that we're the hosts, and they're our guests. That means that we allow the guests to choose first, go first, pick what they want to do, and so on. This was difficult for our children to learn and practice early on, but now it is just a norm in our household that they (typically) abide by. Consequently, they often, but not always, settle arguments by giving in to the wishes of their friends.

Sally Goldberg

That's an easy one. Your job as a parent is to do whatever you can to help your child have the finest experiences every day. One day influences the next, and every minute counts. Arguing produces negative energy, and that is not good. What do you do? Here is the three-part formula:

1. Stop the problem.
2. Figure out what caused it.
3. Teach both children how to avoid the same kind of problem again.

Help each child get redirected in a more positive way. Remember, you are your child's first and most important teacher. When something has gone wrong, it cannot be undone. There is no need to dwell on it. What is most important is for everyone involved to learn from it.

Q My four-year-old is being bossed around by a little girl at school. Though the teachers try to step in when they can, they told me he listens to everything she says. I really want my son to handle this. What can I say to help him deal with this?

Sally Goldberg

Open-ended conversation is the answer for you. Scrunch up together with your child in a favorite comfortable spot, and talk together about lots of things. Whenever you sense it is the right time, ask your son to tell you about that particular girl. Pursue this topic in such a way that you find out as much as possible about what is going on from your child's point of view. Once you understand that well, you will be in the right position to formulate your advice. Because you need to get the most information in the least intrusive way, use language that is both understanding and nurturing. Here are some examples:

- "Tell me more about . . ."
- "How did that happen?"
- "Oh, oh, oh, I see."
- "Uh huh."
- "Good."

Don't ask any questions that could end with a yes-or-no answer, and keep your tone calm and interested. If you start making requests or suggestions before you know the full story, you are likely to meet resistance. When you approach your child from this kind of loving point of view, you should be able to find out exactly what you need to know to successfully guide your son away from this girl's strong, overbearing influence.

Vicki Panaccione

First, I suggest that you find out what your son thinks about the situation. Have a conversation with him: "I notice that Susie likes to tell you what to do. What do you think about that?" See where the conversation goes from there. He may not see anything wrong with doing what she says. Or, he may have a little crush on her and that's his way of getting her to like him. Or, he may be afraid of her and fear repercussions. His response will have a lot to do with the next steps you take.

Here are some other suggestions to help him learn to be less of a follower:
- Give him lots of opportunities to make decisions for himself. Let him make choices, and praise him for making his own decisions rather than doing what someone else wants him to do.
- Practice taking turns at home; you choose an activity and then he chooses the next one.

- Encourage him to take turns at school choosing an activity with Susie. Ask him what he would like to do, and suggest he choose that activity on his next school day whether or not she decides to join him.
- Role play situations in which someone tells him to do something he shouldn't do, and have him stand up and say, "No!"
- Keep the lines of communication open with the school, informing the teachers of the strategies you are using to help him make his own choices so they can follow through at school.

Ilyse Gorbunoff

The big question here is how your son feels about it. He may like playing with the girl and not really care if she's bossy. If that's the case, talk to him and explain that he can be her friend but that sometimes they can do what he likes. Explain that being a friend means that you both make choices. If he wants to be her friend, have her over for a play date so you can observe for yourself and intercede if you have to. However, if he is upset that she's so bossy, then I would see it as a bullying situation and insist that the teachers try harder to keep your son from feeling harassed. Maybe some social-skills lessons or games can be incorporated into the classroom. Some stories about bullying could be helpful, too. I would insist that they speak to the little girl's parents and see what they can do to help her be more agreeable. Explain to your son that he has the right to feel safe at school, and if he does not, he must tell the teacher right away. We don't want to raise tattletales, but we must teach our kids to protect themselves.

Derick Wilder

Being bossy is one of the developmental steps of children, as they are starting to experiment with power. That being said, this can be a serious situation that may require some action by an adult. There are a couple of things his teachers can do. This little girl may be acting out as a result of some of her own insecurities or anxieties. The teachers should see if they can pinpoint some causes and help reassure her when necessary. In addition, their classroom activities should include opportunities for your son and the rest of the children to take leadership roles.

Your son's passive role might be a defense mechanism to combat the unease this situation has caused. One way to deal with this is through interactive play. For example, you could set up a scenario with two toy animals that play together, but one is a little bossy. Remember to keep it light. Have the other animal stand up for himself in a fun, nonphysical way. Beyond role play, your son should continue building plenty of positive relationships with other children, such as classmates, family members, and friends.

Q My daughter is six years old. I have a friend who has a five-year-old daughter. My daughter is very outgoing and athletic. My friend is constantly putting her daughter in the same activities as my daughter so they can be together. The problem is that they argue constantly. My friend says they never argue when they are with her, but I know that is not true, because my daughter tells me differently. I really do not want my daughter and the five-year-old to continue to be around each other. The five-year-old whines and complains, and when she doesn't get her way, she tells my daughter that she is mean. She blames everything on my daughter and tattles about every minor thing. Now, I know my daughter is not perfect and sometimes she is to blame, but she is not a mean child. My daughter likes to joke around, and the five-year-old cannot deal with that. One day I took my daughter and the five-year-old to the mall, and my daughter and I were laughing. The five-year-old got so angry that she closed her ears and shouted in an angry voice, "Stop laughing! I hate the sound of laughter!" It sounds awful, but I truly cannot stand to be around this little girl. I would like to know why she might act this way, and I would also like to know how I can distance this girl from my daughter without hurting my friend's feelings. Thank you so much for any advice you can give me.

Vicki Panaccione

Your question actually has two parts: one has to do with why the five-year-old may be acting this way, and the second is how to handle the situation. Let it suffice to say that any child who hates laughter has some social and emotional issues that will need to be further explored and addressed, probably by a professional. If you are able to have a conversation with your friend about your concerns for her daughter, great! To do that, I suggest that you tell her how much you care about her and her daughter, which is the only reason you are sharing the information. And you might let her know that if the situation were reversed, you would want to know what your friend was observing about your child. If, however, she is not ready to hear what you have to say, then your focus and loyalty must be with your own child.

In regard to your child, it appears that you have given enough time and opportunity to see that this situation isn't going to get any better on its own. Therefore, I suggest that you step in and make the decision that the girls will not be playing together anymore and that you would prefer that your friend not enroll her child in your child's activities. This may hurt your friend's feelings, and that would be a shame. You could explain that you love her and cherish the friendship that you have with her and that you would like it to go on independent of the two girls' relationship.

If she is able to separate your friendship from the issue with the girls, that would be great. However, if she cannot, then you may need to sacrifice the friendship for the sake of your daughter.

Ilyse Gorbunoff

This little five-year-old is probably angry and frustrated by trying to keep up with your daughter. I am guessing that your six-year-old has a more advanced vocabulary, better reasoning skills, and more mature motor skills. By constantly pushing her beyond her developmental level, your friend is causing her daughter a lot of anxiety, and the only way the child knows how to deal with this is by acting out. However, your daughter should not be expected to deal with these outbursts. At six, she cannot understand her friend's frustrations. This is an opportunity to teach her about patience, empathy, and kindness toward a friend. Reward her for being kind and patient when the girls are together.

Additionally, I think what's needed here is some space. Plan play dates for your child with classmates who are a little older, put her in sports and activities that are just for six-year-olds, and try not to be quite as available for play dates with the younger child. If your friend asks why you can't get together, tell her you are having some family time and you will make plans for another day. When the girls are together, try to keep them involved in activities that require your interaction to limit the frustration. Bake cookies, see a movie, or do an art project. As they mature, the girls will be able to be together without fighting. They may eventually be friends, or they may choose not to be close. However it works out, you can still maintain your friendship with your friend if you are careful not to hurt her feelings where her daughter is concerned.

Mark Borowski

It's difficult to say why the five-year-old is the way she is. Learn about how she is being raised by your friend, because it sounds like learned behavior. It's probably best to ask your friend, in a nice way, why her daughter responds in certain ways to situations or things you and your daughter say to each other.

I'm not sure you can distance your daughter from her daughter without hurting your friend's feelings, but I don't think you should worry too much about that. You have to do what you think is best for your daughter. If the mother is truly your friend, then you should be able to respectfully talk to her about the situation. Do basically what you did here. Give examples of situations and how her daughter responded in extreme and negative ways. Tell her you know your daughter is not perfect and that kids in general often respond in overly emotional ways. Explain your concern about the negative effect on your daughter and on the relationship between the two children. Maybe this talk will lead to some positive alternatives. If not, take solace in the fact you addressed the situation in a mature, respectful way, no matter how your friend or her child respond.

Tina Nocera

Sounds as if your answer is in the question. You have to separate your relationship with your friend from your child's relationship with her child. Obviously, this situation isn't working. This often happens as children move from a toddler play-date stage to a slightly older stage and they develop their own personalities and interests. If you have a solid friendship with this woman, it will stay intact. I suggest meeting your friend for coffee without the children. As far as future plans with the children are concerned, don't make any plans or make them far less often.

Q My son, who is five years old, called another child a silly name, which he rhymed with the child's name. We were called up to school because there is a zero-tolerance policy against bullying. I explained to my son about feelings, but really how far does this go? My son was confused and didn't understand what he had done wrong. Have we become so politically correct that our kids can't say anything?

Ilyse Gorbunoff

In kindergarten, children learn so many important social skills, such as how to interact with other children and how to be a friend. Much of this is trial and error. Most early childhood educators understand that sometimes children cross the line, and when this happens they usually can handle it on their own within the classroom setting. I am surprised that this incident escalated so quickly. With that zero-tolerance policy in place, I'm sure the teacher felt she had no choice. I don't want to minimize the importance of anti-bullying and harassment policies because they are necessary and serve an important purpose. I think the problem is that, at the early childhood level, there are no allowances in these policies for normal childhood development.

Continue to talk to your son and remind him about respecting others' feelings. A book or DVD that addresses these issues would allow for discussion and protect your son's self-esteem. I wouldn't want your young son to think of himself as a bully or allow anyone else to label him in this way, especially if this is an isolated incident. Check in with the teacher often, and try to stay ahead of any problems.

Pamela Waterman

I happen to agree that we've gone too far on the PC side, but unless you can get a vote going to change the school rules, you have to help your child deal with the situation. A five-year-old will definitely have a hard time understanding the specifics of how rhyming words (which are a sign of good verbal skills!) could get him in trouble. Good for you for using this as a teachable moment about feelings. You can put this in a broader perspective, saying, "You know how you like chocolate ice cream and some other boy likes strawberry ice cream? Well, children have different feelings, too, about the words you use when you talk about them. You thought that your words were just fun, because you've been learning about rhyming (and that's so clever of you!), but your friend felt a different way. Even if you don't agree, it's nice to stay friends and make your friend feel happy by not saying that kind of name to him." Then, read some Dr. Seuss books with fun rhymes that everyone can enjoy!

Vicki Panaccione

I think this is an example of just how out of control the world is becoming! A five-year-old rhyming a name and coming up with another name is not—I repeat—is not bullying! He probably didn't even have any ill intent. I think it's great that he's learned the concept of rhyming. Of course your son was confused. Rhyming is just rhyming until someone decides they don't like the rhyme. For instance, my name is Vicki. It rhymes with *icky*. If a child had called me *Vicki icky,* that would not have been bullying. That would have been rhyming my name. If, however, I didn't like it, asked him to stop, and he continued to call me *Vicki icky* over and over again, then it would have become teasing and eventually harassment or bullying.

This should never have become an incident where parents were called in. Something that starts out innocently should not be blown out of proportion into a zero-tolerance infraction. It was not an incident about bullying, unless your son was relentless in continuing the rhyme after the other child asked him to stop.

However, you can use this situation to teach your son how to be respectful of others and their feelings. So, for instance, if your son made a rhyme that the other child didn't like, and the child asked him to stop, it's important to teach your son to respect that other child's request. This is a lesson about respect and about things having different meanings to different people. Now, that's a great lesson!

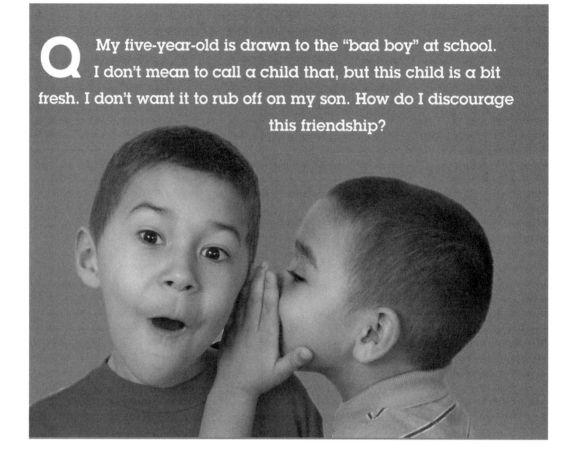

Q My five-year-old is drawn to the "bad boy" at school. I don't mean to call a child that, but this child is a bit fresh. I don't want it to rub off on my son. How do I discourage this friendship?

Rosalind Sedacca

Tread lightly here, and slowly introduce your son to other children with better behavior patterns. Catch him when he befriends or hangs out with another child and praise him, reward him, and acknowledge him. Don't reprimand when he's with the "bad boy," but don't give him attention for it. Children desire positive attention. Your son will slowly move in the direction of that positive attention, but you must be consistent with this.

Tina Nocera

It's interesting how children are attracted to "bad boys." What if your son understood that and wanted to be a good influence on the other child? Our young children have less time to figure out friends than in the past. They are in organized sports and, often, can't go out and play freely. Perhaps that is why we are seeing such a tremendous increase in bullying. We need to give our children time for friends. We can influence what it means to be a good person and a good friend. If you notice your son picking up bad behavior, discuss the behavior, not the child.

Derick Wilder

There can be a tendency for our children to be friends with kids who display behavior that concerns us. Given the wide range of social skills in five-year-olds, you may first want to take a little more time to determine how much of a "bad boy" this other child is. Reach out to his parents and gain a better understanding of their parenting style. Given the dramatic potential of such a conversation, make it a positive exchange and, perhaps, begin by sharing some of your own house rules or disciplinary techniques. Chances are the other parents will reciprocate, and that conversation just might be enough to ease your concerns.

If you don't see the other child's behavior as dangerous, you could just let the friendship run its course for a while. At five years of age, your son may soon move on to other "best friends." At the same time, you can be diligent in reinforcing the traits and behavior you expect from him and pointing out actions that you deem unacceptable.

Ellen Gibran-Hesse

You don't say what else makes this child a "bad boy" other than being fresh. Perhaps you need to relax your judgment. The world is full of people who won't behave to your standards, and your son needs to learn how to handle that. Your son might be curious about this boy and his behavior, which you won't tolerate. You can arrange play dates with children you approve of to encourage better associations, but you can't shield your child from the different children out there. Your focus should be on your son's behavior. If he is respectful to you and your friends, he knows what is right and wrong. If he starts to drift, then you have to set boundaries and consequences. This is just part of learning social lessons. I'm sure he'll be fine.

Q I never expected to have to worry about this yet, but my five-year-old is concerned that her clothes aren't as nice as the other girls in kindergarten. We aren't status conscious at home, so I guess this is coming from school. It's way too early for this. Help!

Vicki Panaccione

Wow! Five certainly is quite young to be so fashion conscious! In situations where your daughter may be grappling with issues at a surprisingly young age, it may be that she has a classmate with older siblings who is prematurely influencing the other children.

Rather than guessing where this is coming from, ask your daughter. Find out what her feelings are about her clothes and why she feels that her clothes aren't as nice as her peers' clothing. She may have seen commercials on TV that have made her want certain brands. One of her peers may have made a comment about her outfit or may have begun teasing her about her clothing. She just may like what other children are wearing or may aspire to be like another child in her class. How you address the issue will depend upon the source of her angst.

If her clothing really becomes an issue for her, it's a great time to begin teaching her about shopping, budgeting, and making good choices. Be careful not to simply dismiss the issue. For your child, this has the potential to make or break her social connections. On the other hand, it's a great opportunity to begin discussing which things really matter, such as personal qualities, and which things are just superficial. Also, discuss with her how there will always be differences among people, which doesn't make them better or worse, just different! You might want to contact the classroom teacher, who may be able to incorporate these issues into some really great teaching opportunities.

Tina Nocera

Congratulations! You've just asked one of toughest questions that have been asked! It shows how challenging it is for today's parents. The outside influences are greater than ever, and they affect younger children. I would turn it around and suggest that your daughter adopt her own style. Use the hype to your advantage; explain how the same people who set styles do so by being themselves. If she is interested, give her a blank book and suggest she "design" her own styles. The important thing here is to help her be herself and not follow others and to have the confidence to express who she is and what she likes.

Ilyse Gorbunoff

Fashionistas develop young these days! Television shows, magazines, advertisements, movies, books, and toys all glamorize fashion and being fashionable. As you walk through the stores, you may notice that the children's clothes are mini versions of the adult department. I'm not sure how you can avoid it. The problem is that you want your daughter to fit in at school, but you also want her to be the kind of person who is not swayed by social status. Explain that, although these things are pretty, in your family you don't buy things just because other people have them. Clothes can cost a lot of money, and your family has other ideas as to how to spend your money, such as on a special family night. With a goal like this in mind, start a special family-night savings jar.

I would not make these items totally taboo, or they will be so glamorized in her mind that she will want them more. Choose your battles. Set a budget, and tell her that she only has that amount each season to spend on items that she can't live without—maybe a pair of boots or special jeans. When she asks for something above and beyond her fashion budget, tell her that you are sorry but she is over her budget. Instead, you will make a donation to the family-night jar. In this way she will have a few items to help her feel more included with the other fashionistas in kindergarten, and you will be teaching her about managing money and sticking to your family values.

Anger, Tantrums, and Tears

Q My four-year-old son has uncontrollable tantrums when he doesn't get what he wants. It's especially embarrassing in places like restaurants or the grocery store. Do you have any tips on how I can calm his outbreaks without giving in to him?

Sharon Silver

The best way to tackle this question is to run a little test to confirm that his tantrums are just that, tantrums, and not a sign of anything else. Try what I suggest for a few weeks. If you haven't seen any changes, then I recommend you read *The Explosive Child* by Ross W. Greene, PhD. If after reading that book and implementing the behaviors you still see no changes, then you might want to see a behavioral specialist. However, your question seems developmentally appropriate to me.

Developmentally, four-year-olds are all about power struggles. They have an unconscious need to learn how much power they have, and the way they do this is to break a rule and see what the result is. When I say *result*, I'm not talking about time-out or punishment. I'm talking about his need to learn what happens in the real world when a person acts that way. He needs to learn that he has to apologize, accept the fact he can't always have what he wants, and fix or repair any damage created by his tantrums.

When he has a tantrum in public, remove him from the audience. I recommend you leave the store or restaurant, but do not go home. Removing him from the audience unplugs the possibility that you'll react because you're embarrassed and stops him from gaining any attention from onlookers. If you go home, you're teaching him that his tantrums ultimately have the power to make you stop what you're doing, proving to him that he's the one in charge.

If you have a shopping cart full of food, hand it over to the manager and tell him you'll be back in a few minutes. Don't be embarrassed; people are silently applauding you for doing something about a public tantrum.

Take the child outside the store or restaurant, and find a place to sit down, maybe on a bench, a curb, or on the grass. Make sure you sit someplace where he can't hurt himself, and just sit silently beside him. Say nothing, unless your silence scares him. If he seems scared, simply keep the talking to a minimum by saying, "I hear you, and I'm happy to talk when you calm down. Do you need a hug?"

Warning: Most likely his tantrum will get worse before it gets better. His increased crying and outbursts are his unconscious way of trying to get you to behave the way you've always behaved in situations like this. Since he's so young, he perceives your previous behavior—yelling and trying to reason with him or leaving—as the normal way Mom behaves. Now that you've changed your predictable response by being silent as he cries, he isn't sure what will happen next and that makes him uncomfortable. He wants to get back to being able to predict what will happen, so he unconsciously does what's familiar to him—he continues crying or whining to try get you to behave the way you have before.

At the first sign of calmer behavior, connect with him and reach out and give him a hug. This next step is where the true learning takes place. Once he's calmer, say, "We need to finish the shopping." Then, ask a few questions related to the specific situation you are experiencing, such as, "Are you allowed to scream and cry in the grocery store? Are you allowed to scream for candy when you don't get it? Are you all done crying? What will you do differently next time? Okay, let's go back inside and finish the shopping."

Asking those questions causes him to shift his focus from crying to remembering the details of what happened in the store that caused you to bring him outside in the first place. Having him restate your family rules helps him understand how the rules play out in a real-life situation.

Janet Price

My heart goes out to you as you struggle with this difficult situation! This has to be one of the most excruciating experiences for parents of young children—seeing our child become uncontrollably angry when he can't have what he wants, and especially doing so in public!

A few thoughts: Remember that behavior is a skill. It sounds like your son does not have adequate skills and strategies to handle frustrations. Age-appropriate behavior comes more easily to some children than to others. Some children need more focus on teaching acceptable behaviors, including how to ask for what they want in socially acceptable ways and how to handle frustrations when the answer is no.

It is important to respond as consistently as possible when your son exhibits unwanted behaviors. Let your son know prior to going out what positive behaviors he needs to have for a successful trip, such as to a restaurant. Keep the expectations simple: "Here are the foods that you can order, and these are not options."

Provide positive comments often at the restaurant when he is acting appropriately. Explain specifically what you are praising: "You are sitting with your legs and hands quiet." "You have been waiting so patiently for our food to arrive." "It looks like you are enjoying the coloring book you brought with you. What a good idea!" "It is so enjoyable to be here as a family and have a nice meal out together!"

If he has a tantrum, be prepared to remove him from the situation—if there is another parent in the picture, one of you can remove him immediately while the other asks for the rest of the food to be wrapped for take-out and pays the bill. At home, it is a little easier to be consistent in not giving in to his demands since there are no people watching. Tantrums are only a powerful tool for your son if they cause the desired reaction in you, such as giving in to the demand or getting your attention. Ignoring tantrums can go a long way to eliminating them or at least reducing the number of times your son employs this strategy to get what he wants. Use words to let him know that you see that he is upset and that when he calms down you can try to find a solution together that works for both of you, such as another toy that is more appropriate for indoors or getting that toy down after nap. Then, walk away (such as to another room) if he is safe, or at least turn away so he sees that his tantrum does not wield power.

Remember that changing behavior and habits takes time and practice. Your son may act out even more at first in resistance to the new ways that you are responding to his tantrums.

Hang in there! Respond consistently and acknowledge any steps you observe in your son toward the positive behavior that you are looking for. If your son does not respond to these strategies, I recommend that you meet with a child psychologist who can assess your situation in detail and offer specific strategies for teaching your son new ways to communicate what he wants and deal more successfully when he becomes frustrated.

Christine Hierlmaier Nelson

Your son may tend toward a feisty temperament. He may be a fun-loving kid ready for adventure; his reactions are big when he is happy and also big when he is angry. Check his diet and be mindful of the things that lead to a meltdown to ensure that his fits are not triggered by sugar, overstimulation, or some other sensitivity. Some kids are more sensitive to light and noise, for example, than others.

Never give in to him when he throws a fit. When you give in, you teach the little scientist in his brain that throwing a fit equals "I get what I want." Imagine that reasoning when he is thirteen! To handle fits in public places, you will have to choose one of three things:

- Calmly finish your tasks as best as you are able while he is flailing around and screaming.
- Leave the store or restaurant immediately and take him home.
- Take him outside or to a restroom and wait until he tires himself out and is ready to listen to reason. If not, you go home.

This is no fun for you, I know. But, I assure you that if your child is otherwise mentally and physically healthy, he will eventually get the idea that he gets nothing from having a fit except a sore throat. To counteract the fits, compliment your son whenever he is behaving well. Tell him that you will add a cotton ball to a jar for each good deed or calm choice he makes. A full jar will earn him a reward. This will support his cause-and-effect scientist in a positive way; he will learn that a full jar of cotton balls equals "I get what I want."

Also, do not pay attention to how other people react to your son. Most parents understand that children aren't always on their best behavior. If they don't understand, it's not your concern. Be the best parent for your child and teach him that screaming does not get rewarded under any circumstances, but you love him regardless!

Sally Goldberg

The solution to this problem is a three-part process:

1. Start at home before you two go anywhere. Explain exactly what kind of behavior you expect. Take the grocery store, for example: He must hold your hand, walk next to you when you get out of the car, and hold on to the cart at all times whenever you are in the store. Tell him that you will let him choose a treat, such as a small pack of crayons to use with you at home, if he behaves well.

2. When you get to the store, review what you expect, and then clearly explain what will happen if your child does not follow those directions: He will not get to choose a treat to use with you at home.

3. Throughout the process, keep mentioning specifics about how well he has been following your directions. Involve your child in the shopping excursion, and make him feel valued, needed, and important. As often as possible, keep pointing out helpful and proper behavior, such as how careful he was getting out of the car. Tell him how much you like having him next to you while you shop. Even point out any good ideas he may have had or any polite remarks he may have made to others. Paying positive attention to your child will be your biggest deterrent to any tantrum.

When you set your child up for success at home, make your expectations clear in the store, and use praise and encouragement in specific concrete ways, you are in control. Tantrums are a way of taking control and do not do well in a prepared environment.

If any tantrum still dares to show up, meet it head-on with love. These new conditions will be your new way to steer your child back on course.

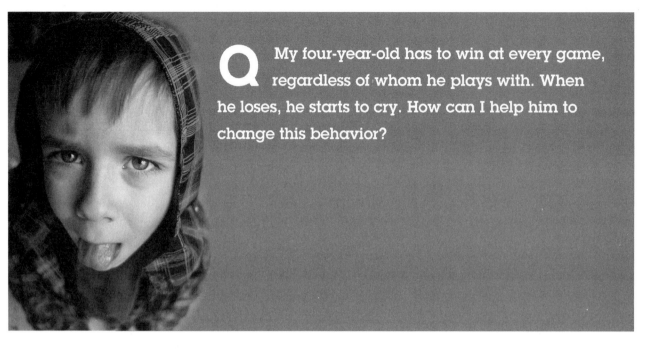

Q My four-year-old has to win at every game, regardless of whom he plays with. When he loses, he starts to cry. How can I help him to change this behavior?

Sally Goldberg

For some reason, he has learned that winning is very important—the goal for playing a game. There are two things that you need to do.

Increase the number of games he plays that are not competitive and in which there are no winners, only opportunities to participate. Try throwing beanbags into a plastic tub or taking turns matching memory cards. There are many more. An excellent source of these is the book *Make Your Own Preschool Games*, available on www.drsallyparenting.com.

If he has to be involved in a competitive game, which I do not recommend under the age of six, take every opportunity you can during the game to point out small successes. As you point them out, use specific, descriptive phrases such as, "You threw the ball far," and "You used two hands to catch the ball."

With these two strategies you should see a big change. Your child will actually experience the lesson he needs to learn: It does not matter if you win or lose. It is how you play the game. More related information is in the book *Constructive Parenting*, also found on www.drsallyparenting.com.

Steven Kairys

Model other behaviors at home with your family. Give praise for effort and not result. Make sure that other family members don't model a win-at-any-cost approach.

Trish Booth

Four-year-olds want to be in control, and that makes winning very important. Explaining that you can't always win and that losers shouldn't cry will not change the behavior. Time and the normal development process will improve his reaction. Until then, minimize the emphasis on who wins. Find creative ways to keep score, such as noting a personal best rather than a comparative best. Praise what he did well in the game, both during play and afterward. Increase the number of cooperative games that use some of your son's well-developed skills. And, ignore the crying as much as you can, and divert his attention to another activity when he starts crying.

Q My son is five. He is having anger issues, and I don't know how to help him. He has always had a problem with this, and it's getting more aggressive. I know all children have problems with not getting their way, but there's got to be a stopping point! He kicks things, shoves things, and hits his younger brother. We've made sure we have quality family time so he doesn't act out for attention. We make sure he gets to bed on time so he has enough rest. I watch the types of food he eats, so that won't affect him. He hasn't had any problems at school—it just seems to be at home. His brother is four years old and in preschool. After school, I am torn between two boys who want all of my attention and who are trying to finish their homework first so they can go play outside. They are still so young; my attention is needed to help them get started. He knows his behavior is unacceptable. We address it every time he has one of his episodes. Please help!

Vicki Panaccione

Your son's escalating outbursts may very well be related to changes that this school year has wrought. Last year, he was the only one in school and the one who commanded your attention at the end of the day. Now, he has to share his status and your attention. Things may be escalating as you each begin to dread his walking in the door, expecting a repeat of the day before. Be careful to greet him each day with a positive attitude and belief in a fresh start. During a quiet moment, perhaps at bedtime, talk to him about his feelings. Let him know you understand that things are different and that it's hard to share you with his younger brother. Ask him for suggestions about how after-school time could be better. The boys are not only competing for your attention but also for who will go out and play first. To stop this, set aside twenty minutes after school when they both have to engage in school-related activities. Or you could work with them one at a time, while the other boy plays inside. No one goes out until the time is up or both are finished, so there is no need to rush. You might ask your older boy to act as your assistant, helping his brother with his "easy" work. This can give him back some elevated status and a way to receive your approval.

Be sure to praise cooperative and independent behaviors; if you only give him attention when he needs help or he's acting up, then he will continue to be more and more demanding. Intervene as soon as he acts up, rather than waiting for his behavior to escalate. Put him in a safe place to calm down. This will let him know you will not tolerate the behavior and will keep him safe. Teach him ways to channel his anger by providing physical outlets such as bop-bags, pillows, or wrestling buddies.

Mark Borowski

My gut reaction is to suggest you consider getting professional help for your son, through a counselor or psychologist. It sounds like this has been a problem for a long time, and it appears whatever you have tried to do has not worked. That being said, here are some things to consider:

- How do you specifically handle his tantrums? I suggest time-outs where he is isolated for a few minutes, followed by a discussion as to the reason for his time-out. Then, have him apologize to his brother or whomever. This is pretty basic, and you may already do this.
- Try to discover why this behavior hasn't happened at school, which might narrow the reasons down to something between your two sons or something specific to home.

- Be effusive in your praise for your son when he does not throw a tantrum or when he handles a situation well. Ask others who care for him, such as family, babysitters, teachers, and so on, to do the same. Regularly explain to him how you or others positively handled a situation without getting angry. Hopefully, these positive examples will eventually make an impression on him and affect his behavior.
- As far as homework after school, consider doing homework with each of them separately. Assign alternating days for who goes outside first.

This will take more time for you, but it may solve the problem of being torn between the two boys. You may be able to work it out at school where the boys are given homework on different days, if the problem is that bad. This might be asking too much of the school, and I wouldn't expect the entire class to switch homework days—just an exception for one of your boys. At that age, my daughter had flexible due dates, so she had a of couple days to get the homework done.

Georgianna Duarte

Sometimes, children experience difficult periods when they are having a hard time expressing their emotions in appropriate ways. However, it seems that your son has had this challenging behavior for a while, so here are some suggestions to help you address this and teach him how to identify his emotions and manage his own angry feelings.

First, try to pull back and observe why the outbursts happen or what event triggers them. Keep a short journal of what precedes each event and what his response is. This will help you focus and identify the strategy that will be most effective. Second, if the behavior is at a dangerous level, safely stop the behavior, calmly pull your son away from the situation, and help him identify the problem. Your calm intervention is critical. Each time he has an outburst, help him find the words to express why he is angry, and reassure him that he has a right to those feelings. There are numerous books to help children identify and manage their anger. Check out the Center on the Social and Emotional Foundations for Early Learning website, http://csefel.vanderbilt.edu. They offer numerous tools, videos, and suggested books to help children learn how to more effectively express their emotions in acceptable ways. It appears that he is frustrated and angry and doesn't select an appropriate way to express it, so now it is a good time to intentionally teach expressing anger appropriately.

Provide jobs for responsibility, and be sure to recognize and provide constructive feedback when he does express his anger in a calm way. These are key ways to let him know that he is valued and that, when he does manage his anger, it is noted. Discuss and create some very simple limits together. Post these in several locations around your house, and gently remind him of them. Be clear about consequences, and make them reasonable and fair.

Mark Viator

The good news is that you have a few options with this situation. Many children do have anger issues that can be dealt with in a variety of ways. Because your six-year-old is not displaying these behaviors at school, we can assume that we are dealing with a boundary issue. It sounds like you are doing all of the right things in making sure he is well tended to. Now it is time to establish some clear and concise rules that reflect the type of behaviors you expect him to display. For example, set a rule that says, "You will not hit or shove." Tie these expected behaviors to privileges that he enjoys. If he takes control of his behaviors, then he can keep the privileges. If he breaks his rules, then he loses the privileges in order from least important to most important. He will lose these privileges for a twenty-four-hour period. Set up these rules for both your five- and six-year-old. Some excellent resources are *Positive Discipline* by Jamie Wyble, LCSW, and *Smart Discipline* by Larry Koenig. The thing to remember with any discipline system is to be consistent. If after a week or two, the behaviors do not go away or if your son begins being aggressive toward others, then I do recommend you take him to his pediatrician or to a child counselor. It is possible that he may be exhibiting behaviors associated with oppositional defiant disorder. Usually behaviors are exhibited toward most authority figures, so his teachers would be reporting these behaviors. This is why I think this could just be behavioral issues associated with getting attention. Try the discipline system, be consistent, and if this does not work, then seek some form of professional counseling help.

Q My three-year-old daughter is not a morning person. I make her go to bed around 8:00 or 8:30 p.m. Just about every morning, I have to fight with her when I wake her up at 7:00 a.m. She screams and pulls at herself for hours. She doesn't give up. Sometimes she screams for so long that she is soaking wet by the time she does calm down. I tried a punishment stool, but she seems to like it. She asks to stay on longer. During her tantrums, she even looks scary. I don't know what to do with her. My husband doesn't have as much trouble with her as I do. I am much stricter with her. I take her things from her to punish her when she doesn't listen. I don't know what to do anymore. Help!

Brenda Nixon

I read several possible issues in your story: temperament, tantrums, discipline, and parenting style. First, it may be her inborn temperament to be slow to warm up. If that's the case, relax and give her time to wake up. Don't talk or try to engage her in an activity for a while each morning. I feel this may be temperament because you said she likes sitting on the stool, which gives her private, undisturbed time and that is what she needs each morning. If your daughter is slow to warm up, it simply means she takes more time to embrace new stimuli or situations, such as a new day. She may never be a morning person.

Second, it's possible her tantrums are just for manipulation. She interprets any attention from you, even negative warnings or reprimands, as attention. If you can ignore her tantrum (providing she's not injuring herself or others), you'll see her begin to calm down when realizes she can't get your attention via outbursts. She does, by your own words, calm down eventually, so she has the capacity to control her emotions.

Third, discipline is about teaching. When she has a tantrum and you give her attention, you are teaching her the way to get you upset is to act out. That's why you should ignore her tantrum. Then, you teach her that you can't be manipulated by her behavior. At her age, she should use words—not behavior—to express frustration. I encourage you to help her use words to tell you what she's feeling. Reading aloud to children is a marvelous way of teaching new words. There are wonderful children's books about emotions at your public library. Check them out, and read aloud to her at bedtime.

Fourth, parenting style often resolves or reinforces a child's behavior. Perhaps when you say, "I don't know what to do," you feel helpless and cave in to her. This further confuses a child. Parents must be in control of themselves and of the situation. If a child senses the parent has lost control, it is frightening. Your husband's style must be different if he doesn't have as much trouble with her. Remember, three-year-olds like to make decisions. If possible, offer her two acceptable choices and let her choose. Don't argue with her decision. Sometimes this is a helpful way to get preschoolers to cooperate while respecting their need to feel independent.

Pamela Waterman

My sympathies! Our oldest daughter is not a morning person. We actually visited a developmental psychologist for ideas when she was three years old, and the psychologist explained that our daughter did not transition well. Lightbulbs went on for us as she said that transitioning from the sleep state to being awake is one of the greatest transitions you can make in a day. Her suggestions: Bring her a small glass of juice, set it at the bedside, and say, "I've brought some juice for you. I'll turn on your music and be back in five minutes." A child's natural blood sugar can be low in the morning, and for our daughter the juice gave her that little jump start she needed. It was also important that we left her to wake up in her own way. You can go back after five minutes and, perhaps, turn on a little light, then leave again. Our daughter would come out after she drank the juice and bring us the glass, but we still didn't try to have long conversations, just the basics about what needed to be done. To this day, she does not want to talk to anyone for at least thirty minutes after getting up. After she gets dressed and gets ready for the day, she is finally willing to communicate.

The book *How to Talk So Kids Will Listen and Listen So Kids Will Talk* by Adele Faber and Elaine Mazlish offers an example of a parent coming in on her three-year-old who is having a tantrum (and Dad doesn't know what to do). The mother brings over a pad of paper and a pencil and says, "Show me how angry you are—

draw a picture of the way you feel." The child draws angry circles, saying, "This is how angry I am!" The mom says, "You really are angry!" tears off the page, and says, "Show me more." He scribbles, and again the mom says, "Boy, that's angry!" They repeat the process, and with the fourth page, he is definitely calmer. He looks at the paper a long time, then on his own says, "Now, I show my happy feelings," and draws a smiley face. He goes from angry to happy because the mom lets him show how he feels in a way he could manage—with a pencil—and she simply pays attention.

Many times it works to ignore them, but perhaps in this case, you can just watch. So, juice, a little soft music, and some time to get going on her terms—I hope these ideas help. Remember, a lot of adults are not morning people, and they have to come from somewhere. Oh, is she heading to a daycare? (Ours was.) If so, perhaps setting a timer will help, if you're on a schedule. Hearing the timer go off can work better than hearing you say, "Time to go."

Beverly Willett

Sometimes the terrible twos strike at three. Have you asked your pediatrician if her behavior is normal? If so, she'll probably just outgrow it. When my children were little, family members used to tell me that children that age were prone to doing the opposite of what you'd tell them to do. Your daughter probably realizes you don't like her tantrums, hence her ability to get to you by acting out. They don't seem to bother your husband, so she doesn't bother using her tantrums to get his attention. Children break away from the nest little by little throughout their lives, and your daughter may simply be starting to assert her independence. The next time she pushes your buttons, try not to get upset. If you feel you need to put her in the naughty chair to reinforce that the behavior is unacceptable, by all means continue. But, don't worry about her reaction. Concentrate on yours. Go about your business, take a deep breath, literally count to ten, and see what happens. Most likely, this too shall pass.

Q I have a twenty-month-old daughter who is starting to throw fits whenever she doesn't get her way. She really knows what she wants; for example, if she doesn't want her diaper changed, she will twist and turn and make life very difficult. I have tried explaining that I don't like her behavior. I have tried ignoring it. I have even given in a few times. What is the best way to handle this situation?

Norman Hoffman

You have to know what this child wants the most. For example, most children are very unhappy when they are deprived of their parent's attention, even for a minute. If that has a great effect on your child, you may use that as the stimulus to remove the target behavior of throwing a fit. Stop trying to explain to her the virtues of behaving well. Stop ignoring her behavior. Take charge and give her an opportunity to either choose to behave or lose your attention for a few minutes. You may have her go to another room, which prohibits her from seeing or hearing you. After two minutes, go to her and ask if she is ready to comply. If not, have her remain for another two minutes. Repeat this method until the behavior changes. Most young children enjoy play and the attention of loved ones. When either is removed, that can become the catalyst for change of behaviors.

Georgianna Duarte

A twenty-month-old child seeks autonomy, and these are important opportunities for her to stretch, express, and twist and turn. The good news is that her twists and turns are her independent efforts to declare, "This is my body!" Honor those expressions, and use language to let her know you are trying to understand. Encourage her to use language to express herself. Ignoring is a very effective strategy for dealing with the negative behaviors, but it must be done consistently with love. This is difficult to do, so self-talk to soothe your own spirit in the process. In terms of her diaper change, try a consistent song, provide new and creative simple toys she can hold in her hands, and respond calmly to her twists and turns until she realizes this is a soothing time.

Sharon Silver

Twenty months is the beginning of the terrific twos, a time when everything is about opposition, frustration, fear, and anxiety. The conflict for a two-year-old is wanting two things at once and not knowing how to choose between them. A good example would be a child who is conflicted about whether to visit the doll in the next room or Mom in the kitchen. She can't decide. Then, she becomes anxious because she can't decide. She gets frustrated at her indecision and sits down and cries. Mom rushes in to try and make it better, and the child becomes obstinate and has a full-blown tantrum. As the tantrum progresses, the child gets fearful because she doesn't know how to calm down and is too young to express that to Mom, so the tantrum gets even bigger. Mom doesn't know what to do because helping seems to upset her and staying away seems to upset her as well.

You can see that being a two-year-old is about being introduced to options, control, and power as you're experiencing overwhelming emotions, fear, and frustration. It's best to assign words to what she's doing: "I see you're scared," or "Wow, you're angry!" Then, tell her, "I'm happy to hug you when you're ready."

When it's all over, go back to doing what you need to do, such as changing her diaper. It's best to wait to discuss her behavior until the tantrum or squiggling has subsided and she's calm. Don't try to get through to her while she's upset. You'll know she has begun this stage when she shrieks and says, "I do it!"

My suggestion would be to give her some power or redirect her as you change her diaper. Either let her get the diaper, let her look at a book, or talk about what she gets to do after she's changed, instead of talking about the squiggling. Realizing that you don't like being changed is the very first step in potty training. She hasn't shown enough signs to be ready for potty training just yet, but the first piece of the potty-training puzzle has occurred.

Two more tips. From now on, diaper her on the floor so she doesn't roll off the changing table. And, try changing her while she's standing—that may help. Moving fast and using an excited voice to redirect her is key with any child at this age.

> **Q** My seventeen-month-old has slapped my face twice in the last week when I was doing something he didn't like, such as putting on his jacket or changing his diaper. He yells, "No, Mommy, no!" and wham! right across the face. I've never hit him, and he hasn't witnessed hitting at home. Where did this come from, and more important, how can I stop this behavior?

Brenda Nixon

Even when tots grow up in a peaceful, nonviolent home, they often go through a stage of aggression. It's most common around the age of two years. My suggestion is to watch out—if you see his little paw coming toward your face, reach out and intercept it. Hold his hand and firmly state, "I am not for hitting." Then, continue your work with him. If he repeats, you repeat. He must learn there are boundaries. If he insists on slapping at you, then I suggest a brief moment of passive time-out. Simply look away (no eye contact) or turn his body away from you. This sends a brief message that his consequence for slapping is no contact from you—the most important person in his universe (for now).

Trish Booth

Your son could have seen someone slap another person outside your home, such as in a store. Or, it could have been a spontaneous gesture that he has repeated because he got a reaction from you. Your son is starting a normal developmental phase of exploring and testing limits.

The challenge for you is that this phase can be quite frustrating because, as part of the testing, children repeatedly do the things they aren't supposed to and become provocative. That being said, it is important that you set a limit and forbid hitting.

The next time he makes a move to slap you, try to avoid the contact. Immediately say in a sharp, stern voice, "No. No hitting." Then, calmly proceed with what you have been doing. Many parents try to do a lot of explaining about why not to do unwanted behavior. However, at seventeen months, a short "No. No hitting," is more effective. Don't be surprised, though, if he immediately tries to slap you again as you resume the behavior he doesn't want. If he tries to hit again, simply repeat, "I said no hitting." After your reprimand, it's best to give him some control within the behavior you are continuing. For example, offer him a choice, such as, "You need to have a clean diaper. Do you want a diaper with ducks or bears on it?"

As your son gets older and more verbal, you can work with him to use words rather than hitting to express his feelings. But, for now, you are helping him understand the boundaries of acceptable behavior.

Vicki Panaccione

It is very common for toddlers to hit when angry or frustrated. At seventeen months, your son is beginning to strive for independence. He can now walk and talk and is beginning to do things for himself. The last thing he wants is to be constrained or overpowered. Any effort on your part to contain him in any way–such as putting on a coat or changing a diaper–can be met with resistance. It is easy to take the behavior personally, but try to understand the message behind it. Hitting is telling you he feels too constrained or is feeling a loss of control.

Since he has already hit you a few times, I suggest that the next time you need to change his diaper or put a coat on him that you communicate with him ahead of time. For instance, let him know that it is time to change his diaper and that you notice lately this has been a problem. Ask him how he would like to help you in the diaper-changing act. Give him some autonomy in the process: Let him hold the diaper or the ointment, hand you the wipe, and so on. In this way, you are not simply taking over but involving him in the process. Recognizing his feelings ahead of time and working on a solution may solve the problem.

However, if he tries to hit you again, it is important to stay calm and remain in control. Hold his hands together so that he can't hit, say "No!" in a stern voice, and let him know that hitting is not allowed. You might try saying, "Ouch!" or "Owie!" and making a sad face so he understands that hitting hurts. Encourage him to help you in the process, rather than fight you. A few don'ts: Please don't hit to punish hitting. And, don't ignore hitting. It should be dealt with calmly yet firmly.

Q My son is three and has not been feeling well this week. He has gotten upset with me about having to get dressed or something simple and has tried to hit me. I put him in time-out. Is there anything else I should have done?

Jill Wodnick

It is a tricky balance deciding when boundaries need to be clearly set and when a little body needs more support. As you said, your son was not feeling well and was responding inappropriately, or so we are ascribing. Is it possible that his resistance to getting dressed has been a greater need for snuggles and sleep? I am not a big fan of time-outs; I believe your son needs to know how his behavior made you feel and then needs to make amends. Using warm baths, snuggles, and extra floor time playing together is another way to give him more quality time and redirect his body.

Steven Kairys

If he is sick and not feeling well, then be supportive and ask him, but also help him. Be empathetic and caring. Look for signs of frustration, and redirect him before he loses his temper. Give him positive strokes for the little things.

Brenda Nixon

It could be a passing thing—there are days I don't feel like getting dressed, too. At three, your son has the motor and cognitive abilities to dress himself. I encourage you to offer him two acceptable outfits, let him pick, lay the clothes on the bed, and walk out of the room. He is responsible for dressing himself, just as he'll be when he's in school. Avoid turning a simple morning routine into a battle of the wills, which will put you both in a bad mood and start out a new day in an ugly way. Rather, make mornings lighthearted. Another fun thing to do is to "race" him and offer to see who can get dressed first. This always worked with my daughters, who are now older and dressing themselves.

Q My two-year-old throws a tantrum every time I put her in the car seat. What can I do?

Tina Nocera

What makes this a challenge is that we have to take children in and out of car seats as we run errands. Is it possible to schedule errands after your toddler has napped, eaten, and had a chance to play? Try to group the errands so they are close together, so you may be able to use a stroller rather than the car.

Ilyse Gorbunoff

Some things are nonnegotiable, and car seats are one of those. I would insist that your two-year-old sit in her car seat, even if she's upset. If you can make the investment, it might help if you go to the store together and let her choose a car seat she likes. She may be more willing to sit in it. If that's not a feasible option, maybe she can pick out a special blanket or small pillow to put in the car seat to make it more comfy. Also, I would get some special music or audio books that you can both listen to, but only after she's buckled in. Make a big deal out of it, and tell her what's going to happen: "First, I'm going to buckle you in, and then we're going to listen to *The Three Bears.*" A special car-only stuffed toy or special snack also could be helpful. Praise her every time she gets in her seat without a fight, but never let her win this battle, even if she screams. Safety has to come first!

Vicki Panaccione

There are many reasons why a two-year-old may throw a tantrum when put into a car seat. The most common reason is because she's two and she wants to do it herself! If, in fact, you are picking her up and trying to put her in, her tantrum may be her declaration of independence. Try asking her to get in herself. You might play a game, such as to see who can get in their seat and buckle up first. Kids this age are fiercely independent and welcome the opportunity to do things for themselves.

If the crying isn't about independence, you may want to make sure that the seat is comfortable, her legs aren't pinched, the straps aren't rubbing, and the buckle's not too tight. Additionally, some kids do not like forward-facing seating, so you might try turning her around again. Here are some other suggestions to avoid tantrums:

- Never start the car without her in the seat and buckled. No one goes anywhere until everyone is safe.
- Before going to the car, talk with excitement about where you will be going and how anxious you are to get there.
- Pick out a toy, book, or snack that your daughter can only play with or eat in the car once she's in her seat and buckled up. This provides an incentive to get buckled in.
- Be sure to give lots of praise when she cooperates with you.

Q My son is two-and-a-half years old. Overall, he is a well-behaved kid except when it comes to transitions. He has a fit when it is time to leave any social outing such as the mall, gym class, restaurants, or play groups. He cries, drags his feet, kicks, flails his arms, and sometimes lies on the floor. I am seven months pregnant, and it is becoming increasingly difficult to carry him to the car and strap him in his car seat when he is behaving like this. When we arrive home, he sometimes has another fit from the car to the house. Before we leave any social outing, I always give him a few warnings, letting him know we are getting ready to leave. I don't know what else to do. I am so frustrated and feel like I need to be confined to my house with him. I know that is not the solution. He never behaves this way for my husband. When he is out with my husband, he does complain about coming back home, but he has never gotten physical or had a tantrum. I don't enjoy spending time with my son outside the home anymore.

Michelle Maidenberg

First, if it is only happening with you, note that certain dynamics are being played out, and it is obvious that he has the ability to do generally well with transitions when he wants to. A little bit of complaining is developmentally appropriate. From the sound of it, you would welcome having to deal with just that reaction. I encourage you to watch your husband and son's dynamic when he is transitioning. Try to understand what might work best with your son, what he responds well to, and what dynamics have been created that get in the way of transitions.

Use positive reinforcement for his successful achievements. Pay attention and recognize when he is able to hold his own and transition well without being physical and aggressive. If you have just been giving verbal warnings, he may not understand that a change will take place. Try saying it first, then ask him to put on his shoes and then his jacket. Finally, let him get his goody bag and say goodbye. Congratulate him on each step to reinforce his cooperation through verbal support and recognition.

Trish Booth

Transitions are often hard for toddlers and preschoolers. Parents and children can easily fall into a pattern of a child meltdown. You are on the right track about giving him warnings that it will soon be time to leave. Unfortunately, two-and-a-half-year-olds don't have a good sense of time. The key is to have a structured plan to move him through the transition:

- A notice
- An activity he has control over
- A definitive end
- A transitional focus

Try limiting yourself to just two warnings. The first one is just an announcement, "We will have to leave in five minutes." After this announcement, do anything you have to do to get ready to leave. Then, in about two minutes (or when you are done getting ready yourself) say, "It's almost time to go. What do you want to do before we leave: go down the slide or swing on the swing?" Give him the choice of only two things to do. After that activity, state firmly, "Now it's time to go." Take his hand and start moving toward the exit. You may be able to head off a tantrum by giving him a task, such as carrying something, looking for the car in the parking lot, or talking about an upcoming event. "Its lunch time. We're going to have spaghetti." Be sure to praise any cooperative behavior. Although children often behave differently with each parent, you might be able to use some of your husband's techniques or phrases. Ask him to describe how he handles transitions. It may also help to explain your expectations just before the activity itself. "We have to leave right after gym class. When the class is over, you'll need to put your shoes on and go out to the car. I expect you to get your shoes on when the class is over." Then, follow that routine at the end of gym class. The hard part is sticking to the routine. It will take many times of responding firmly and sticking to the plan without using empty threats or bribes for him to learn that tantrums aren't as effective as they once were. When your son realizes that he will leave when you say so, his tantrums will diminish even though his verbal protests may not. Finally, some of what is driving your son's behavior may be your pregnancy and the changes that has brought. This can make your son push boundaries as he tries to find the new limits. If you feel that your relationship is beginning to center around tantrums, take a few extra minutes of quiet or cuddle time each day to enjoy being together.

Georgianna Duarte

Transitions are difficult, and if they are not predictable, smooth, and said with a calming voice, they can be problematic. Try using puppets, songs, and rhymes to help him make those transitions. Don't respond to the negative, since watching it is reinforcing the behavior. Calmly prepare with objectives, a busy bag of activities, and a song. This should decrease the transition phase. Turn all media off, including cell phones, so there is a great deal of time to talk, exchange ideas, and an opportunity for him to express himself verbally.

Janet Price

This is, indeed, a concerning situation. We all assume that bringing a child into our lives will bring wonderful new opportunities for being in the world, not hamper it to the level you describe. Being seven months pregnant must add to your frustration on many levels—the exhaustion of pregnancy and the expectation and need for your son to be more independent. Then, to top it off, your son does not give his father as much trouble as he does you. That may occur if your son spends the majority of his time with you. Dad might be someone who is a little more novel, someone to be on better behavior with. Observe your husband's approach with your son in these moments. Is it something you can replicate or at least approximate? One key piece to remember is that when you implement a new strategy for encouraging positive behavior, it is very common for the unwanted behavior to actually increase before it begins to subside. So, when trying a new strategy, give it a week or two for positive results to take effect.

Have your son's struggles around transitions become worse during your pregnancy? If so, this may be a relatively short-lived problem. My guess, though, is that these struggles were occurring before this pregnancy. These may be skills your son lacks. So, for the present, you will need to be his support for surviving transitions. He needs to know that you are in charge.

I recommend that you start by reducing the transitions in his day to a bare minimum. Pick outings that have the most hope for success. The goal is to shape positive behavior for your son around transitions. That means providing positive, specific praise whenever you observe the desired behavior—for example, "You came when I called! Good for you" or "Thanks for getting into your car seat and letting me buckle you in." Try playing games as transitions approach, such as counting the number of steps it takes to get from the play group to the door of the house or from the door to the car. Another game that can distract from the actual transition is to pretend to be an animal as you walk from the mall to the parking lot—"Let's be bunnies and hop, hop, hop to the car!" "Let's be as quiet as a mouse leaving the restaurant, tip-toe, tip-toe." That greatly reduces your need to make these already stressful situations into ultimatums, such as, "Get in the car, NOW!" "Stop whining in the restaurant," and "No hitting Mommy!"

I notice that the examples you give here involve noise (the mall, restaurants) or groups of children (play group, gym class). Your son may be struggling with the demands inherent in social settings. His ability to process sounds, activity, and movement around him and your expectations for his behavior may be a significant challenge for him, one that causes him to become so overwhelmed that he cannot access the appropriate behaviors that he is able to exhibit in less stressful situations. If you find that your adaptations for successful transitions are not working, consider taking your son to a child therapist who specializes in behavioral challenges. The therapist can let you know if he would benefit from an evaluation for sensory struggles (aversions to loud noises, for example). That closer look into what is causing your son to handle transitions ineffectively might be illuminating.

As difficult as things are at this moment, you are on the right track in looking for ways to help your son handle transitions more successfully so that you can enjoy outings with him now and when your new little one joins the family.

Q My two-year-old exhibits defiant behavior, primarily to his mom, who is his primary caregiver. This behavior includes throwing food at dinner, kicking and throwing objects at mom during diaper changes, and hitting when he is frustrated or does not get what he wants. We have been unsuccessful in our attempts to find a way to curb this behavior, especially the hitting, which is unacceptable. We have tried time-outs, but we aren't convinced they have helped. Many of these things began at a fairly early age. He began having temper tantrums around ten months, and he began hitting around fifteen months. The behavior has gotten more frequent now that he is two. Thankfully, I have been told he does not do this at day care, which tells me there might be more that we as parents can do to change this. While I understand that he is two and likes to push buttons, I am uncomfortable with the point we have reached. I welcome your thoughts.

Charlotte Cowan

The behavior you are describing in your child sounds fairly typical for a two-year-old, and I am reassured that at day care your son is fine. I suspect that at day care they offer the structure and consistency that are often hard to keep up at home, especially if the parents disagree at all about how to handle a given situation. Your day care might have some tips for you since they know your son. In this age child, unacceptable behavior needs to be addressed calmly and firmly every time it happens, when it happens. "Wait until I tell Daddy" or "You're going to your room when we get home" are entirely ineffective. Instead, almost regardless of the offending behavior, the child needs to be warned once that this behavior is a bad idea and that he needs to stop. Then, if he does it again (which he will), he needs to be interrupted, told again, and moved, usually by carrying him a few feet away. Place him on the floor and leave, assuming that the spot where you have put him is babyproofed. Give him a pillow to hit if he is mad. Tell him that he may join you again when he is ready to stop hitting, throwing food, or doing whatever behavior you are trying to address. He may try to join you while he is still angry and will need to be carried out again. This approach takes work but will be effective—as long as all caretakers involved are consistent. Children this age need to be *expected to* rather than *asked to* behave. Sometimes it is hard for parents to remember that they are in charge! By consistently setting limits and by modeling the behavior they are seeking in their child, parents can win these battles with even the most stubborn two-year-old!

Trish Booth

Learning self-control takes a long time. It is especially difficult when a child must use actions rather than words to express needs and frustration because he doesn't yet have the vocabulary. You can help with that by naming for him what he is feeling and helping him use words to express it. Parents often have to remind children to "use your words." For a two-year-old, a time-out is simply time away from the situation. Your son is not yet old enough to think about what he did. If the time-outs don't work because he immediately repeats the forbidden action, it is better to remove or change the source of the problem. If you mean that time-outs don't work because he is still doing the behavior despite many time-outs, that is typical for a two-year-old. You may even go through the phase where he does the forbidden action and then puts himself in a time-out. That demonstrates he understands the action is wrong but doesn't yet have the self-control to not do it. For temper tantrums, it is easier to just walk away from them as long as your son is in a safe place. You can also carry your child to a safer place, such as his bedroom, and then leave. It is hard for a young child to maintain a tantrum when no one is watching. Because it is hard to walk away from a half-changed diaper, you may want to reward his being cooperative. You can use a very small snack or special attention, whichever works best with him. If your son is throwing food at dinner, consider making that the end of his dinner. That means calmly announcing, "You're done when you throw food," and taking away all food and utensils. If you still want him to sit with you at the table, give him a quiet toy to play with. Children who are hungry rarely throw food, so he was probably done anyway. If he is throwing food at the beginning of the meal, consider that he may be overtired and hungry before the meal starts. It may be better to have him eat earlier and join you at the table for only a small amount of food followed by a quiet activity. Children often act better at day care. His day care provider may have very clear rules about behavior and consequences. Ask what these are, and consider having the same rules and consequences at home to give him consistency. This may not completely solve the problem, however, because children tend to regress when they are in the comfort of home.

Brenda Nixon

Two-year-olds go through a developmental phase where they are more aggressive and defiant. It's not pleasant, but it's normal. Part of it is because they have powerful feelings, but they lack the words to express themselves. Part of it is to get attention if they feel ignored. Part of it is to manipulate their world and get what they want. Here are two suggestions to help you during this turbulent but short phase: First, read books, recipes, mail, road signs—anything to your son, to surround him with words. This will teach him language, and eventually he will be able to use words rather than his body to express emotions. Second, be a model of self-control, to teach him how to calm himself. Therefore, don't yell, spank, or do other behaviors that may teach him to yell, hit, kick, throw, and so on. Little ones watch parents and learn from them, even when the parents don't know they're being watched.

Sibling Rivalry, Family Issues, and Life Changes

Q My middle child is five years old and struggling with feeling left out. His older brother, eight, finds him annoying and often chooses not to play with him. The five-year-old has become very whiny.

Steven Kairys

Middle children often have a hard time fitting in and feel like they are not getting enough attention from siblings and from their parents. A lot depends on their innate temperament and their personality. The quiet, more timid children have the hardest time gaining attention.

Certainly do not respond to whining, but try to proactively work out some positive approaches. Help him gain some self-confidence, create activities for him and his friends, plan some one-on-one parent time with each child, and also plan family time with all the children. Ask the children for their suggestions at a family meeting.

Vicki Panaccione

Middle children can certainly struggle to fit in—they are too young for the older sibling and too old for the younger sibling. Check to see if he is getting lost in the lineup.

Help him find a defined role and purpose in the family, and help him identify all the things that are great about being his age and a middle child. It is not your eight-year-old's job to entertain him! However, the older child is not allowed to be mean to him either. If your oldest wants to have a friend over or have quiet time, he needs to be allowed to carry on with his eight-year-old life.

Your five-year-old needs to learn to entertain himself, and he also needs to be encouraged to have friends and activities of his own. Often, the younger siblings spend too much time wishing they were the oldest and wanting to do what the oldest is doing. On the other hand, it's perfectly acceptable to create some family or sibling time in which the kids are required to interact. You might ask your oldest to spend some time with his brother, with the understanding that he only has to do it for a set amount of time or for a specific activity. If he is forced to do too much with the younger one, he will begin to resent his sibling. So, be careful that he isn't forced to show too much brotherly love.

One final comment: Be careful not to give in to whining. When you do, you are actually teaching your child to whine. If he is whining about something, don't just tell him not to whine; encourage him to say it in a different way.

Ashley Hammond

Like all children, middle children crave attention and compete for the focus of both parents and siblings. Encourage activities that all three children can be involved in, but be sure to offer ideas that allow each child to work at his developmental level. Painting together, building blocks, and fun games will allow the eight-year-old to be "boss," but the five-year-old can enjoy them and learn to help.

Whining is really a call for attention, and it needs to be addressed with a combination of cooperative group play and time to play by themselves. Giving each child small-group, fun activities can encourage independence and help them be less dependent on you and the older brother. Surf the web for activities for groups and individuals. These can provide ideas for simple fixes for the whining. You can also build an arsenal of fun things to do!

Q My children, ages four and six, seem to fight all the time, and I end up in the middle. It is exhausting, and I had a different vision of what it would be like having two boys close in age. This isn't fun.

Tina Nocera

Here is how I got out of the middle. It's a technique that worked so successfully for me that the teachers asked why my children (twenty months apart) got along so well.

I realized that most of what we do as parents is referee. That means we are making judgments, but we're doing it without the facts. I decided I would no longer be the "bad cop." I decided to take myself out of the game. We started "child of the day" at our house when our kids were even younger than yours.

Basically, child of the day is a very simple system of responsibility and rewards. Each day you mark on the calendar who is child of the day. When it came time to decide what story to read, what movie to watch, or what snack to eat, the decision went to the child of the day. That was the reward part. The responsibility part was that the things that needed to get done but were not necessarily a particular person's chore belonged to the child of the day. For example, if I need something out of the pantry, I would ask, "Who is child of the day?"

This approach took me out of the middle. Now, my children are both adults, and if you ask them who the favorite child is, they will both say, "Me!" This really works.

Pamela Waterman

I feel for you—I have three daughters, each two years apart. At first, it was the older two, at ages six and four, going at it, and then it became the middle and youngest when the oldest was in school. I did step in if I overheard chaos that was clearly escalating. I agree, it's exhausting, but I set some rules. I said, "I can't be with you both all the time to see what is happening or who did what. If you can't take turns/share/agree on what to play with, I will have to decide for you, and I will take turns as to who wins—whether you like it or not." I made sure each had alone time, as well as together time. We put names on everything that definitely belonged to one or the other, especially gifts. Also, I set up boxes and shelves for each one's special toys and art supplies and created a shared toy and art-supply center.

If they couldn't "give" on something, then neither one got it. And if they really went at it, I separated them, which soon made them both sad as, ultimately, they wanted to play together. Down the road, when the six-year-old starts doing more things with his own friends, then you will need to step in and make sure the younger one has his own activities and distractions.

Sally Goldberg

Here is the parenting principle for you—Set up for Success. Once you have that down pat, you will be on your way. The underlying reason for your troubles is sibling rivalry, and that is actually a positive survival mechanism for your children.

Given that, evaluate your trouble spots and see how you can better set up conditions for your boys so that they find it easier to behave well. Here are a few possible improvements you might be able to make. Use any of these that work for you, and then create others to fit your needs.

- Divide all toys by color, and use that distinction as an arbitrary way to settle toy disputes quickly and fairly.
- Make a five-minute rule for some toys, and include a timer when necessary.
- Designate separate areas in your playroom or house where each of your children can have total control.
- If coming home from school is a problematic time, arrange it so that each of them arrives at a different time. Depending on what your situation is, use whatever resources are there to help you—after-school care, an activity for

one child or the other, playing at a friend's house for one of them, or some other creative way for you to be able to give one-on-one time to each child.

Yes, it is very hard to keep giving your full attention to two children who need it at the same time. Once you get a handle on setting up your home environment for success, you will be able to avoid almost any kind of confrontation before it starts. You will be well on your way to having the fun you always wanted.

Rosalind Sedacca

Usually when siblings fight constantly, there's an underlying competition between them. One may feel he gets less attention or is favored, or he just may be jealous of the other's skills and attributes. As a parent, you can pay attention to make sure both of your children are feeling loved, valued, appreciated, and accepted. Note if you admonish, dismiss, or punish one more than the other. Spend individual time with each of your sons so they both feel your love without competing with the other. Have your boys come up with consequences that they've agreed upon in advance to see if that doesn't help shift the energy, as well.

Q My son is two and half years old and has suddenly become very aggressive and stubborn after the birth of our second child. It's been almost three months, but things are not getting better. He resorts to shouting, hitting, and even harming the baby. What to do?

Pamela Waterman

It's the classic resentment and bewilderment at having to share his parents' attention, which was never the case before this "crying lump" came along. You do have to keep explaining that hitting and harming the baby simply will not be tolerated. But, you can let him draw a picture to show you how angry he is (even just dark lines on a paper help get out the feelings). You could also tell him, "How about you growl as loud as you can when you feel like that?" Tell him, "I'm glad you showed me how mad you are. Whenever you feel that way, come tell me and I'll give you a hug." A great book on this topic is *Siblings without Rivalry* by Adele Faber and Elaine Mazlish. Look at pages 32–35 to see other examples of strategies to try.

Vicki Panaccione

First of all, you need to keep the baby safe. Be sure that your son does not have unsupervised access to the newborn under any circumstances.

That being said, your son's behavior is very typical when a new baby is born. Up until the time of the new baby's birth, he was the baby and getting all the attention. I suspect that he is very jealous and angry because of all the attention the baby is being given. The attention given to him has probably dwindled, except for when he acts up!

Remember that your two-year-old is very much still a baby and needs lots of attention and reassurance. Think about it: All of a sudden someone else is getting most of mommy's and daddy's attention, and the toddler is being treated as a "big boy" and expected to fend much more for himself. He is not any older than he was before the baby was born, and he needs lots of love and attention regardless of the baby! Just because you are happy to have a new bundle of joy doesn't mean your toddler sees it the same way.

My suggestion is that you validate his feelings by recognizing that it's probably hard or not fun to have a new baby in the house. Commiserate with him about the baby crying, how much attention the baby is getting, and so on. Give him permission to dislike the baby, but set firm limits: "It's okay not to like the baby, but it's not okay to hurt the baby." Let him know that you would not let anyone hurt him, and you won't let anyone hurt the baby, either.

Spend one-on-one time with him daily. If he gets aggressive during the day, remind him that your special time together is coming right after nap or dinner or whenever you have it planned. Pay attention to him in various ways, not just as the new big brother. Keep his routine as regular as you can, just like he had before the baby's birth.

If you give him lots of positive attention and validate his feelings, his frustration will diminish and, I believe, so will his negative behaviors. Once he's not forced to like or love or even accept the baby, he will come to do so in his own time and in his own way.

Trish Booth

Two-and-a-half can be a stormy time even without a new baby in the house. Here are some suggestions to deal with the several things that may be going on.

First, he can't harm the baby. He needs a consistently enforced rule about how he treats the baby. Tell him you know he is upset and doesn't like it that the baby is getting fed or held (or whatever the issue of the moment is). However, he can't hit, pinch, poke, or otherwise hurt the baby. Enforcing that rule with some kind of a time-out will give him (and you) a few minutes to calm down.

Second, he needs time each day to burn off some of his energy. If he can't go outside to use his big muscles, do some active play inside. Play music and dance, stomp, jump, and wriggle to it. Doing this activity with him can actually be a stress reliever for both of you.

As for his shouting, try the approach, "Yelling hurts my ears, so I can't understand you. You'll have to whisper." Whispering it to him can both get his attention and model a lower voice level. Sometimes loudness is an effort to make up for lack of words. If he is just shouting without saying words, try giving him the words he needs. You can say, "You look angry. Are you angry?" Giving him a place to shout and blow off steam might also work. Choose a distant corner or closet. (If you use the closet, only open the door so he can shout into it. Don't put him in the closet.)

To address some of the rivalry, which is normal, make sure that you give him special time each day. This is time when just the two of you do something that he enjoys. If it comes toward the end of the day, you can talk about looking forward to that time. If it is earlier in the day, you can remind him of something positive about the time you had together. The amount of time can be short, fifteen to twenty minutes.

Finally, give your son things to do that he can be proud of. Suggest tasks he can do now that he's a big brother. This can include getting a diaper, toy, or other item for the baby. He can entertain the baby by singing, telling a story, even "reading" one of his favorite books aloud. You can do this sitting together on the sofa, while you hold the baby so that you can closely monitor the interaction. Be sure to praise your son whenever he shows kindness rather than aggression. That will help him build on his positive interactions.

Brenda Bercun

Adjusting to a new baby is a challenge for everyone in the family, especially a toddler. It is very hard to share mommy's and daddy's attention. The bottom line is that you want your son to learn that his new role in the family is very important, not only to you but also to the baby. Being a big brother is very special, and there are many ways to reinforce this.

First, I would make sure that your older son's needs of playtime, proper sleep, and nutrition are being met. Make special time with him when the baby is sleeping. This time can be either playing with him or having him help you with simple fun chores, such as sorting laundry. Always praise him for his attempts and successes. Verbalize that he is a wonderful helper and that you had fun with him.

When the baby is awake, reinforce their budding relationship by pointing out to your older son that the baby likes him and likes looking at him. When the baby learns new skills, such as smiling, praise the baby and congratulate your older son on being a wonderful teacher to the baby in teaching the new skill: "The baby learned this from watching you. You are a wonderful teacher and big brother. The baby is lucky to have you, and so am I."

When you are feeding the baby, have a special basket of toys and books that your older son can use during this time. Let him know that this toy basket only comes out during feeding time. Every so often, change the toys around so that he won't be bored with them. If possible, either sit on the floor with him while you are feeding the baby or be at the table where he will be playing. Compliment him so that he knows you are paying attention to him.

Encourage your son to be a helper when appropriate, having him carry an item for you, get something you asked for, and so on. Make sure your son feels appropriately acknowledged for his good behaviors.

With these changes, the aggression should decrease and, hopefully, stop. But, if your son is aggressive to the baby, I would encourage you to give him a short time-out by having him sit on the floor or in a chair for about thirty seconds to one minute. I would then invite him over and help him express himself, if possible. Maybe he needed a hug from you, is tired or hungry, or the baby was crying and he didn't like that. Helping your older son develop words and expression for his needs is an important part of emotional development. When your son is calm, explain to him that hitting is not allowed and that if he hits or shouts at the baby, he will get a time-out. But, if he tells you what he needs, you will do your best to help him. Explain that, as a big brother, he is not allowed to hurt the new baby. It is the job of everyone in the family to make sure everyone is safe. Make sure you reinforce the smallest of positive interactions. Hug him, high-five him, give him a thumbs-up. When he knows that you are catching him at being good and reinforcing the behavior, you will see more of it.

Q I am a single father. My son is four years old. Recently, my child's mother and I had a falling out. She has gone to stay with her mother and rarely calls our son. From what I hear from his teachers, there has been a small change in his behavior patterns. He is doing things that are out of character. How do I best explain a complicated situation to a four-year-old in order to keep his spirits up at a time I know is difficult for him?

Ashley Hammond

As you correctly point out, this situation is complicated and, by definition, is probably not going to make sense to your four-year-old, no matter how well you explain it. I would recommend discussing this situation with his mom and working quickly on a good visitation schedule. Your son just knows that he is not seeing Mom, and this is tough for any child.

Work on the behaviors at school as a separate issue. Children can and do function very well if they have a stable home, even if only one parent is present. Your love and stability will be crucial at this time. Firm and loving guidance on behavioral issues with your son and firm discussions with his mom may bring some short-term pain but long-term growth.

Mark Viator

While this may be a difficult situation for you and your son, you may be surprised how well your son will understand. The first thing that I recommend is to keep your explanation simple and honest. Second, do not place any blame. Do not degrade yourself or his mother. Let him know that you and his mom are not getting along well right now, but even though this is happening, you both still love him very much. This reassurance is what he really needs. If his behavior continues to be a problem at school, take some time to talk to his teachers. Let them know that he is going through some changes at home. His teachers can be a great source of consistency and reassurance for him also.

Ilyse Gorbunoff

This is not an easy situation for you or your son. I think the keys here are patience and time. It will take time for him to adjust, but he will. Kids can handle a lot more than we give them credit for. As long as he feels safe and loved, he will be okay. It is great that you are communicating with his teachers. Continue contact with them so they can give him a little more attention and understanding. If he acts out in school, talk to him and be honest. Tell him you understand he's mad and that he has a right to feel the way he does, but we still have to follow the rules. There are consequences for these behaviors even though we understand why they are occurring. The loss of a privilege or a time-out is not mean. Continue to discipline him as you would have before this loss, or his behavior will get out of control. He may not know why he's angry, but he is. Putting words to it may help. Be as honest as possible, and say something such as, "Mom has gone to visit her mommy, but she's thinking about you every day." Try to keep his schedule as normal as possible. The routine will help him understand that everything is okay. Try not to give him extra things to make up for what he's going through. This will compound the problem and reinforce that something is wrong. Spend extra time together doing fun things to keep his mind and body occupied. Trips to the park, watching a favorite video, and cooking together will help. Make Mom a journal in which he can draw a picture to tell her about his day. Drawing his feelings or thoughts of her will also help. At some point, he can send it to her or just keep it for her until he sees her. Perhaps he can send her a nightly email, but if she doesn't answer that's okay. He can just give her a quick update of his day or say, "Goodnight. I love you." Most of all, try not to let on that you are angry. Let him talk about her if he wants to. At bedtime, tell him how much you love him and that, even though Mom is not here, she does love him, too. Reinforce that none of this is his fault.

Q My husband and I recently divorced. My child's teacher now tells us she sees some new behaviors at school that concern her. He is hitting and biting! He doesn't do this at home, but seems to be trying to hurt children at school. What should we do?

Jill Wodnick

It sounds like your child's teacher is seeking to partner with you, which is great! Work with the school to see if they participate in Rainbows Group, www. rainbows.org, which supports children going through a parental divorce. Outside of school, work with a play-based social worker or family therapist to give everyone tools for communication and greater functioning. Your son is going through a major transition. Offer deep empathy and compassion but set clear behavioral boundaries. Work with the school and use community resources and perhaps faith-based services to honor your family's needs right now.

Rosalind Sedacca

Pay attention immediately. First speak to the teacher and then to a child psychologist, who can advise you about this. New, aggressive behaviors following a divorce usually indicate a child's frustration, anger, guilt, or other emotion regarding coping with his new reality. Catching these behaviors early makes it easier to address the issues and give your child the attention, clarification, scheduling adjustments, and emotional support he may need at this challenging time. Don't focus on punishing your child for misbehavior. Focus instead on communicating to find out what he is feeling, who he is angry at, what he would like to change, and how you can find a win-win solution to ease his pain. This, of course, is not always easy, especially with a young child. That's why professional assistance is such a blessing. They usually use play therapy to get the answers you want, and often a child will communicate more candidly with a therapist than with his parents when life at home is stressful.

Ellen Gibran-Hesse

You don't say how old your child is, but I am assuming he is in elementary school. My youngest son was ten years old when I went through a divorce. He behaved amiably, but his grades went down and his teacher saw changes. This is a time when I think it is best to take your son to a therapist. I chose three and then let my son pick the one he felt most comfortable with. At first he resisted, but eventually he formed a very strong bond with his therapist. Your son may need a third party to let him vent, so he isn't doing it at school, and so he won't fear alienating you. Young children don't know how to channel their emotions, and a therapist can help him. That way, your son won't feel he is putting you on the spot.

Beverly Willett

Is reconciliation possible? I'm sure it's difficult to hear this, but my hunch is that divorce is the culprit. It would help, though, if I knew how old your child was, more about your divorce, and whether you and your husband are able to co-parent. A family breakup is really hard on children, and the negative consequences of divorce are well documented. Unfortunately, many parents believe that if divorce will make them happier, their child will naturally be happier, too. Unless yours was a high-conflict marriage or an abusive one, however, children aren't necessarily better off. Family counseling for you and your family is probably a good idea. Since I don't know how old your child is, I don't know whether your child might also benefit from private counseling. I also recommend reading up on how divorce impacts children, including a particularly good book called *Between Two Worlds* by Elizabeth Marquardt.

Christine Hierlmaier Nelson

Children don't always know how to express what they are feeling when there is a major change to their routine, home, or family. You can provide reassurance that it isn't his fault and make sure to spend time with him, but he may still act out with anger and confusion to seek comfort for his feelings. Give him a constructive way to show his anger, such as a punching bag or permission to yell at the top of his lungs, when appropriate. Tell him it's okay to feel angry. Apologize for the change, and promise you will still be there for him, no matter what. If the behavior continues, you might consider family therapy to help him express how he feels and learn better ways to cope. The sadness and anger of a divorce can linger in children for years; be proactive now to help your child recover from his loss. Also, take care of your own health so he can continue to count on you.

Q My child is two and a half years old. Her mother lives in another state and has sporadic contact with my daughter. My daughter has begun to bite the other kids in her day care, and no matter what we do, it keeps getting worse. Her pediatrician said that she needs to be spoken to and removed from the situation. This is not working. How can I get my daughter out of this habit? My daughter lives with me, my father, and brother in a small apartment. We moved in here out of necessity, and it is crowded. We have only been here a few months. We will be moving to Florida within the next three weeks, and she will have more room and a big back yard. I believe that the day care is not equipped to deal with this type of situation. My mother suggested a child psychologist, but I am not positive that it is a good idea to put another person in her life and then take her away. I am trying to make her life as stable as possible. When her mother is around, she is drunk, so I think I may have to stop the visits. I am thirty-one years old and currently work full time. My daughter is well behaved for the most part. She does not throw many temper tantrums anymore. Any help would be greatly appreciated. My goal is to teach my daughter, not to berate or diminish her.

Beverly Willett

It sounds like there is a lot of stress and change in your life right now. Children sense frustration, too, and biting may be your daughter's current way of dealing with hers. For now, I'd suggest following your pediatrician's advice, and give it time. Sometimes it takes more time than we, as parents, think it ought to take, but each child is different. Consistency in handling the matter is key. Make sure that you tell your daughter no when she bites. Try giving her a time-out whenever she bites; suggest the day-care center do the same. Be firm, but try not to get angry. Given what you've told me, it doesn't sound like rushing off to see a child psychologist is warranted right now, especially before you move. Also, while your daughter is probably too old to be teething, check that out with your pediatrician, just to be sure. If she is, your pediatrician should be able to suggest something that will soothe your child's gums. When my teenage daughter was little, she was a biter, too. We thought she'd never grow out of it, but she did. Looking back, it's funny how one day it just seemed to go away. With kids, I've learned that, more often than not, the problems we think will never disappear become a faint memory over time.

Part of your daughter's acting out may be tangled up with how she's feeling about being separated from her mother. You may know your ex as a "drunk," but she's still Mom to your daughter. The situation must be painful for her, and at two-and-a-half, she can't use her words to tell you what she's feeling. So, just love her and be patient.

Finally, remember that your daughter's biting doesn't mean you're failing as a parent. On the contrary, it sounds like you have your daughter's best interests at heart. Keep it that way, keep loving her, and try not to worry. My thoughts go with you in your upcoming move.

Steven Kairys

If she only bites at day care and not at home or with other children in other situations, then there is something at the day care that is increasing the frustrations. Usually, immediately removing the child and using a time-out do work. Provide a lot of praise when she doesn't bite in a situation where, typically, she usually does. Try to understand what provokes the episodes, and then try to anticipate and divert her attention before the biting occurs.

Ellen Gibran-Hesse

You are to be commended for taking a positive attitude toward your daughter. She is going through a lot. You may be right to restrict visits by her mother. You don't say how often your daughter sees her or if the visits seem to go well for the child, if not for you. It is hard to know what the seed of the problem is, and I wouldn't want to remove the mother if she brings some love to your daughter. Still, your daughter may be upset and angry not to see her mother more often, especially when she leaves. As soon as you move and get settled, you may want to take her to a child psychologist or see if the change in day-care environments does the trick. In the meantime, I would sit down with the day-care staff to see if you can work out a plan. Find out if there are triggers for the biting, and perhaps institute a small reward system for when your daughter goes all day without biting. A sticker or small treat would do, something she can look forward to and that the staff could remind her that she is working toward at the end of the day. Good luck on your move.

Q Hugo is thirteen months old and has had one nanny in New York for nearly all of his life—until four months ago. We moved to Boston, and we have had trouble finding a suitable full-time nanny for him. We've let two go and are now on our third. I'm not sure if it's his age (entering into toddler stage) or the instability that the nanny situation has created, but he's becoming a very, very whiny and unhappy child. He seeks my attention constantly and cries every time the nanny comes. (And she's really nice!) He's not even super comfortable with his daddy anymore. In addition, he is teething his back molars. I've tried ignoring his loud whines and cries to no avail. I've tried catering to him, and am now I'm resorting to scolding him loudly, which seems to quiet him (but sometimes upsets him as well). I don't want to be habitually raising my voice to him and using a negative tone. I simply don't know what else to do. He will start his baby care school in one month, which I think he will enjoy. But with his recent behavior, I'm worried about his adjustment there as well. Any advice will be so appreciated.

Jill Wodnick

Good for you for acknowledging and recognizing the effect changing caregivers is having on Hugo's emotional and physical body. Hugo's job is to be biologically programmed to want you more than anyone else, no matter how nice the caregiver may be, so he is truly doing his job by seeking your attention and deep connection with you.

I encourage you to commit to four twenty-minute check-ins of floor time with him each day for fourteen days. Use the timer if you need to, and commit to not answering the phone, being on the computer, making the bed, or any other task. Even when he starts the baby care school next month, continue the floor time with him. Use sensory materials such as blocks, playdough, or uncooked rice in a plastic container; look at board books; sing songs; and truly be present and available with him.

If you do this protocol four times a day for twenty minutes each time, I think you will see him become much calmer as more of his emotional needs are being met by you in his space and with materials that serve him. Have fun when you try this, and remember how much I admire your willingness to submit this question.

Trish Booth

The move and the changing nannies could be a source of stress that is fueling the whining. Your son is at an age where he wants you to be near him. Leaving or inattention can trigger a scene that your son hopes will bring you back to him. You are right; scolding him is not a good long-term strategy. Here are a couple of suggestions to help him whine less. First, try hard not to reward his whining. When he is whining, calmly explain to him that your ears can't hear him when he is whining. If he wants you to hear him, he has to talk nicely. Model the volume and tone for him. Then, as soon as he speaks more normally, reward him by telling him, "I can hear you now that you are talking nicely." You don't necessarily have to give him what he wants. You just need to tell him that you can hear him. Throughout the day, reward your son by commenting on his nice voice when he is not whining. In the beginning, it can be hard to repeat over and over that your ears can't hear him. However, if you are relatively consistent, he will catch on. Talk to his nanny privately. Ask her what she does when he whines. Try to come up with a plan so that the two of you do pretty much the same thing. The consistency will help your son.

It is important to consider your son's temperament when you introduce him to the baby care school. Does he charge into new situations, or does he need to hang back and observe for a while? Plan to give him the time and support he needs to adjust to this new situation. Talk about the new things he will see and do. If he is people oriented, emphasize the people he will meet. If he is a train or car enthusiast, talk about those toys. At the school, connect him with what will be of greatest interest to him, as soon as possible. One-year-olds don't really play together; they parallel play. That means it is easiest to set him up with his own toy near another child. You may want to be the one who helps him with the transition. Or, if he has developed a better relationship with the new nanny, it may be easier for her to be the one who takes him. With this arrangement, he doesn't have to give you up to join the others.

Steven Kairys

Thirteen-month-olds that are this troubled are unusual. I wonder if there was some trauma with one of his caregivers that scared him. Children who are stressed or have had some trauma either act out or regress and become withdrawn. So, first stabilize this environment so that it is consistent, nurturing, and safe. Praise the positives, and ignore the negatives. Catch him being good. Anticipate the bad times and redirect. Don't raise your voice. Instead, try some humor and kindness. If the episode is too much for you, make sure he is safe, and you leave the room for a while. Since children at this age do everything for attention, don't get caught up in giving him the attention, even if it is negative.

Christine Hierlmaier Nelson

Sounds like Hugo has experienced a lot of instability with his care providers and your move to Boston. Even at his age, he can sense change, and it's scary. That is why he is clingier or whinier at the sign that Mom or Dad is leaving him. Rest assured that he will recover, especially after his teething pain has improved and you keep a consistent nanny and routine. In the meantime, spend lots of time with him at meal times, bath and bedtime, and during other routines so he gets a sense that Mom and Dad are there for him. When you do have him stay with the nanny or send him to school, keep that routine just as consistent—up at the same time, dressed and fed, kiss and hug, and goodbye. Scolding, lingering, and hushing will only prolong his confusion and not allow him to settle into his new surroundings and feel comfortable with new people. Eventually he will find security in this new environment and with his care providers. Make sure you are a constant in the routine, and he'll feel secure with you, too.

> **Q** I'm fortunate to have my in-laws care for my toddler while I'm at work, but we don't agree on a number of things. For example, I don't like the TV on, and they have it on all day. But my son is there, and I don't want him watching. How can I address this without causing a problem?

Beverly Willett

I don't think there's any way around addressing this frankly with your in-laws. They're doing you a big favor; so acknowledge that up front when you sit down to talk. This is not to say that you're being unreasonable. TV shouldn't be a substitute babysitter, and children need other stimulation.

If you can't afford day care or a private caregiver, you'll have to be prepared for some give and take. Before you sit down, make a list of your biggest concerns. Then, list the other things that upset you but that you're willing to let slide. You might even ask your in-laws for their suggestions first, so they feel like they are really part of the process of working this out rather than viewing you as just complaining. Perhaps begin the conversation with, "I can't thank you enough for taking such good care of your grandson, which allows me to go to work to earn money my family needs." Follow up with something such as, "Now that you're retired, I can appreciate, too, that you like to enjoy your TV. But, my pediatrician says children Tommy's age should watch less TV and spend more time playing, looking at books, and interacting with caring adults. Tell me what I can do to help us work this out and still make things easy on you."

Vicki Panaccione

When it comes to having relatives watch your child, it is important to pick and choose your battles. It sounds as though your in-laws are doing you a great service by watching your son while you're at work. And, while you don't want to bite the hand that feeds you, you would like them to do things your way. You can request certain things from them, but they probably are not going to change their whole lifestyle just because your son is there.

Take a look at the things you object to strongly versus the issues you would prefer be different but you could let slide. Then, together with your spouse, have a talk with your in-laws about what you would like them to do and why. For instance, they might not be aware that little ears pick up everything they hear and that some of their TV programming may not be appropriate for your son to be exposed to. Also, recognize that things have changed and that the way they raised their kids may not be the way of this generation. Keep the lines of communication open; otherwise, resentments can fester. An atmosphere of tension or hostility is certainly not good for your son.

And remember, if you cannot agree or compromise on key issues, you may need to find child care elsewhere and limit your in-laws' time with your son.

Ilyse Gorbunoff

You are fortunate to have in-laws who can help you in this way. Being cared for by family members at this young age has so many advantages; it may be worth some flexibility and compromise when it comes to your ideas on child care. When you approach the subject, try to do so in a way that is not critical of how they do things. Perhaps, say that you read an article that says a daily schedule is an excellent first step in preparing a child for preschool. Tell them that, now that your son is getting a little older, you would like to try this, but you need their help. Together, map out a daily routine that will work for all of you. Include a specified amount of TV time, acceptable foods, duration of naptime, outside play, and so on. Hopefully, if they do not think you are criticizing their way of doing things and feel as if they are helping in the plan, they may be more willing to follow it.

Q My grandson, who is just over two years old, has recently started to become upset when his mom leaves him. The first occurrence happened at a fitness club, when she left him with a caregiver. Up until now, he has never been in the company of anyone other than family. I'm hoping that he will become more used to staying with others but wanted to see if this is somewhat normal.

Sally Goldberg

Life today has terribly confused parents. They think that putting their child in the care of others is often preferable to being with his parents, grandparents, other family members, and close friends of the family. While it is not preferable, it is often necessary. Therefore, there are ways to handle the situation so that the child will receive the nurturing love, guidance, support, and protection he needs. To answer your question, yes, he will become more used to staying with others, and yes, this is normal. Continue to provide positive family time to give him the security he needs to adjust to the care of others when it is necessary.

Amy Sherman

It is normal for children that age to be afraid of strangers. This should change as the child becomes more socialized. Mom should stay with him in the new environment for a while, so he feels safe. Perhaps Mom and the new caregiver can play with him together so he sees that this is all fun and there is nothing to fear. It may take some time to adjust, but eventually he'll be fine being left.

Ilyse Gorbunoff

Separation anxiety is very common; nevertheless, it can be very upsetting. My children had a terrible time with this, so I know firsthand how hard it is on the child and the parent. Some children run off and play, while others cry until they make themselves sick. It just takes longer for some children to handle the separation. Tell his mom to plan to return to the fitness club. Before they go, let him choose a toy or stuffed animal to bring with him. Remind him that he is going to stay with the caregiver and that Mommy will come back. Tell him this several times along the way. Tell him what fun things he can do while he waits for her to return. When they get to the fitness club, suggest that she spend some time getting him settled in, let him show his toy to the caregiver, and help get him engaged in an activity. Then, when she's ready to go, give him a quick kiss, remind him she's coming back, and tell him something they will do together when she returns. Finally, she should go do her workout, but keep it short—maybe fifteen minutes. Each time they go, she can make it a little longer. Before long he'll be able to handle the separation.

Q My five-year-old is begging us for a dog. My concern is that we both work outside the home, and the dog would be another chore for us to tend to. Life is stressful enough. How can I explain that to him?

Jill Wodnick

You have clearly defined why a dog would not work in the rhythm of your home. As much as your son wants to hug and pet a dog, it is simply not a realistic option for your family. In the past, I have taken my young sons to our local animal shelter, where we brought cat food and they were able to sit and pet the cats. Another way of giving your five-year-old access to animals is through a zoo.

I urge you to keep your voice steady and consistent so the harmony of your home is honored. Children love animals. It is wonderful when pets work, but not every home should have a pet.

Pamela Waterman

Oh, the pet question—what parent doesn't face this at some point? You are so right to be concerned about the work and stress. With an older child, you could point out the expense and time involved. However, for this age, tell him that a dog would be so unhappy to be left alone at home all day with no one to play with or to take her for a walk. Dogs love to run and play, and the evenings just wouldn't be enough. You can also tell your child that you know he loves animals very much and would never want to make them sad. If there's an animal shelter near you, perhaps the two of you can visit once a month to donate some food or old towels and blankets. Tell him that this is a way he can make many dogs happy all at the same time. Maybe when he is a really big boy (like someone you know who is twelve or older), he could help after school with dog care.

Ilyse Gorbunoff

I am a great dog lover, and I think kids learn a lot about caring and responsibility from having a dog. However, at five, your son is really too young to help or to learn these lessons. You are right; a dog does add a lot of stress and work to a family. It's like having a baby that never grows up. There is also great expense with pet ownership that many do not consider. Tell your son that, when he is older, he can get a dog. Then, he will be old enough to walk it and help you take care of it. Tell him you are not saying no, but you are saying not yet. Tell him that you are too busy right now and that it wouldn't be fair to the dog. Read books together about different kinds of dogs and about caring for dogs. Tell him you are learning all you can so that you will be great dog owners when the time comes. Look into doing some family volunteering at an animal shelter, so he can spend some quality time caring for dogs. If all else fails, you can start off with a smaller pet, such as a fish or hamster. It probably won't make him forget about the dog, but it will distract him for a while.

Derick Wilder

In this case, while your son may very well want a dog (a very common request), it sounds like your lifestyle just would not support the addition to your family. So, you are definitely making the right decision in not giving in to his request. Too often, after the honeymoon period ends, families either end up with a neglected pet or one they have to get rid of, neither of which is a healthy situation.

I think honesty is the best policy in this case. Gently break it to your son, and give him a simple explanation in terms he can understand. If he continues to really want a pet, and you think one that's low maintenance might be right for your family, consider an alternative. Some good options include a fish, a bearded dragon, a corn snake, a turtle, or a rat.

Christine Hierlmaier Nelson

As you expressed, a dog is a huge responsibility and shouldn't be considered lightly. If you, as parents, aren't ready for the responsibility, it's not right to bring a dog into the family to satisfy a child. If you're worried about your child thinking you are meanies or that you've deprived him of a childhood experience, just remember that you've done the right thing for everyone, including the dog. Tell your son that he has plenty of years to adopt all the animals he wants someday; tell him you'll even visit his zoo! Take him to visit the dogs of friends or family so he can explore this interest.

Q In a world of obligations, my husband and I find that we are lying to family and friends to avoid commitments from taking over all our free time. The problem is that our kids hear us and now think that it is okay to tell little lies— not the message I meant to send. How can I be honest and not hurt anyone's feelings, which is something I would love for my kids to learn.

Elinor Robin

Each of us has to prioritize how we will spend our time, money, and other resources. Each of us is happiest when our time, money, and other resources are spent in alignment with our goals. It's okay to block off appropriate time in your calendar each week as family time. If the time is blocked off with a purpose, it will be easier to tell a caller that you have already committed that time. The irony is that your friends and family members will be less insulted with a declined invitation than they will be with uncovering a lie. But the big issue here is not offended relatives. You do not want your children to grow up believing that lying is okay (or they will lie to you). Instead, you want to teach your children to be true to themselves and their priorities; otherwise, they will succumb to peer pressure. Children learn what we teach them. Our subtle, indirect lessons are the most significant teachers.

Eleanor Taylor

Children learn family values in many ways, but the most powerful way is watching adults and imitating them. If you want your family to value honesty, then you must show integrity in how you handle difficult situations without lying. If you tell lies, even small ones, you can set the stage for your child to feel it is okay to avoid pain by not telling the truth.

At times, when we anticipate that being honest will result in hurt feelings, we are afraid to tell the truth. But, there are ways to explain difficult decisions to other people honestly and openly. Your current situation is a good example. With people who you know well, you can politely turn down invitations or requests by explaining that your family needs a time-out from being busy. Or, if that feels uncomfortable, remember that you are not obligated to tell someone why you cannot go somewhere. Saying, "Thanks so much for the invitation, but we cannot make it," is all you really need to say.

Watching adults be honest in all situations will give your child the courage and the skills to handle his own hard situations in the future, including being able to tell you the truth.

Pamela Waterman

I hear you about all the time commitments with school events, plays, rehearsals, music lessons, sports practice, and so on. You just want to use your down time for quiet, house cleaning, and family fun—not another obligation! You can say, "I know you've heard Dad and me tell Uncle Dave we're busy next Saturday, even though you know we just told you it's time for a do-nothing day. We've always raised you to be honest, and this must be confusing, so here's the way we see it. We love our extended family and friends, but our first obligation is to be a strong family, just ourselves. With all the schoolwork, activities, and job requirements we juggle, it's important and it's the right thing to do to put our needs first once in a while. Having said that, we also don't like to say or do anything that is a lie, but we have to balance that with not hurting other people's feelings. We like to be with them, but it doesn't always work out. You'll get to where you can judge for yourself about when it's okay to say you have other plans. This is part of what people call polite society, and you will see that standing up for yourself can be done nicely."

Ellen Gibran-Hesse

It is hard to say no, but that is a healthy lesson for your children to learn. Tell family and friends that the time is being reserved for family and that you are so sorry to miss the event. I have friends who are very religious and will not answer their phones on the Sabbath. Once the rule is established, people will generally respect it. Your rule is that family time is not to be displaced, whether it is a spur-of-the-moment or planned event. It is more important to honor family than please others. Be polite and firm. You may need to talk to your husband about structured family time so that you both are on the same page. Confusion responding to family and friends can come across as rejection. This will teach your children they can be honest and honor time for themselves and, eventually, their own families.

Q We try to teach our son that he can't have everything he wants. But, when his grandparents come over, they totally disregard our rules and buy him whatever he wants and even leave him money. My husband agrees with me, but they don't listen to him, either. What can I do?

Tina Nocera

Grandparents have good intentions and like to shower their grandchildren with gifts. But, I can appreciate your concern about material gifts and suggest that you begin to invite the grandparents on some outings. You could do simple things together, such as visit the zoo, go apple picking, plan a trip to the playground, or other activities that require little money. What the grandparents will begin to learn is that enjoying an activity lasts a lot longer than the momentary pleasure of a gift. After you have a few of these experiences, you might take it a step further and invite them to dinner and show pictures and talk about the fun. Over time, the change in behavior should have a lasting, positive effect.

Amy Sherman

This is a very common problem for parents. As kindly and as gently as you can, tell the grandparents your concerns about spoiling your child. You want to first let them know how much you appreciate all they do for their grandchild and that you know they love him. However, when they give him whatever he wants, you feel he does not understand the value of a special gift. Therefore, if they can please give him their love, attention, and quality time together and save the gifts for occasions, he will not always expect something from them and will appreciate a gift more when he gets it. Remind the grandparents that you didn't get everything you wanted. It's been a long time since they parented!

Rosalind Sedacca

Don't stress out about it. If the grandparents have been told and have disregarded your requests, minimize the time they spend with your son but don't end the relationship. Many grandparents believe it's their place to spoil the grandkids. They relish their time together and get great pleasure from buying gifts and leaving money behind. This behavior, much as you may not like it, won't negate your parenting messages and lessons. It's just part of having grandparents, which is a very special relationship. Just keep up your own parenting, especially in alignment with your husband, and don't sweat the issue too much. Be happy that your son has the blessing of loving grandparents in his life.

Ellen Gibran-Hesse

This is a hard lesson for parents to learn. You can't make the world adhere to your parenting style. Aside from that, you seem to be confusing spoiling and giving. The relationship between a child and grandparents is very different from that of parent and child. Their time with their grandchild is limited, and they want to celebrate being a part of his life. A good way to handle this is to teach your son to write thank-you notes for his gifts. Even if he can't write, he can draw a picture and you can write the thank you. He'll learn how to appreciate a gift and his responsibility. You didn't say how much money he is given, but this is a great opportunity to show him about saving. Have him put half of it away in a savings account, and let him spend the rest. My sons had small allowances, beginning when they were five. Of course, initially they blew it all, but then they wanted the next new toy. I told them they had to wait for their next allowance or learn to save. It didn't take long for them to learn how to save, but they also got good at shopping for deals. To this day, at ages twenty-four and twenty-seven, they shop sales and outlets. Look at this as a great opportunity to give your son some great life skills and a wonderful bunch of memories with his grandparents!

Discipline, Manners, and Setting Boundaries

Q My daughter is fifteen months old. She's biting. It's not aggressive—she does it when she's happy or excited. She has been doing this for a while, but she is also getting her first molar right now. Is there a way to teach her not to do this? And more generally, what are appropriate forms of discipline for her at this age? In most cases, I can tell her no, and she'll stop doing what she's doing. If she does not listen, I remove her from the area. But for some things—like the biting—relocating her doesn't exactly have the same effect.

Vicki Panaccione

It is very common for a toddler to bite, particularly when happy and excited. And if she's teething, it will feel good and will relieve some of the soreness. She has been biting things for most of her life without incident; she does not understand the difference between biting a person and biting an object. She has to be taught. So, even saying no can be confusing unless you really make it clear that it's not okay to bite a person, but it is okay to bite objects. You might try saying, "Ouch!" or "Owie!" firmly and calmly, and make a sad face so she understands that it negatively affected you. You may also want to redirect her to a different, chewable object. "No bite Mommy," followed by offering a replacement object is much more effective. In this way, you are simultaneously correcting one behavior and replacing it with another. This is a key to disciplining kids at any age: When telling and showing them what they can't do, show them something they can do instead!

Steven Kairys

Be consistent. Redirect her immediately to other activities. Give her positive feedback when she is in a situation where she would ordinarily bite but does not. In general, for a fifteen-month-old, try to predict when she might have issues and redirect her. Ignore those behaviors that you can ignore, and give a lot of attention for the behaviors you want.

Trish Booth

It is normal for infants and toddlers to use their mouths to explore the world. This can lead to nonaggressive biting. You can help her stop doing this by telling her, "No. Don't bite." Then, help her redirect her energy and enthusiasm. Teach her to substitute another activity for biting, such as clapping her hands or making a sign or gesture that indicates she is happy and excited. You can also give her a word to say. Even if she doesn't immediately start saying the word, this will help in her transition to using words to express emotions.

As for discipline in general, you are doing the right things by saying no to unsafe or unacceptable behaviors and removing her from those situations. There may be times when you can divert her attention or redirect her actions ahead of an unwanted behavior. At fifteen months old, your daughter still needs you to monitor and stop behavior that is unsafe or unacceptable.

Q My five-and-a-half-year-old son strongly resists throwing away wrappers and packaging, saying that he can make something out of it later. I find stashes of ice-pop sticks, toy packaging, and so on. He also doesn't want to pass on clothing that is too small. What might be going on here, and how can I help him feel more comfortable in letting go of things?

Pamela Waterman

I know that stashes can drive you crazy—the look of the mess, the possible bug attraction—but your son must be wonderfully creative! Get a special plastic bin with a lid for him, and find a place for it in your house, perhaps in a designated craft cupboard. When he has something he wants to keep, tell him that if it's clean, he can keep it if he puts it there and only there. If you find it anywhere else, you have the right to throw it away.

Maybe you could also do a craft with him, perhaps gluing his favorite wrappers on construction paper and making a card or a sign for his room or for a gift. You might also buy him a box of craft sticks as a substitute for the used ones— tell him it's hard to get food and possible germs off the used ones, so you're giving him clean ones. Regarding the clothing, it can just be hard to let go of old favorites—that's normal. Start by having him give one item of clothing away whenever you buy one new one. If he's really resistant, just quietly pack away a few items and see if he even notices. I did that with seldom-used toys. If no one asked about it after three months, I gave it away. When my children reached about age seven, I also had them come with me when I donated surplus stuffed animals (not their favorites at all) to a home for abused children so they could be personally thanked. They liked that!

Trish Booth

Some people are born collectors. Help him limit his collection by getting a storage container made of plastic or nylon mesh. Use one that will hold only slightly more than his current stash. Then, explain that it's fine to collect things, but there has to be a limit and the limit is what will fit in the container. Anything beyond that or stashed in other places will be thrown away. The first few times he loses what isn't in the container will be difficult; however, he will learn to choose and properly store the items that are most valuable to him.

Perhaps having a family clothing drive would be helpful. Talk about the value of helping others by passing on clothing that no longer fits. Go through your own things, and choose what needs to be passed on. Talk about the happiness you will bring others when they get this clothing. Then, together, sort his clothing. If he can't do this and declares each item his favorite or something he needs, stop the activity, saying you'll do it another day. Later, take away the too-small items when he isn't around. Keep them out of sight for a few weeks so that he gets used to them being gone. Then, pick a day to pass on the family clothing. Put the box in the car so you both can take it to a shelter or nonprofit organization. If he begs to keep the clothing, suggest he keep one item as a remembrance of when he wore that size. You choose the item and casually talk about why it would be a good one to keep—having him look through the box to select the item will only remind him of all he is giving away. After this first giveaway, keep a box in his closet to put clothing that doesn't fit. You can create a small ritual of putting items in the box when you discover they are too small. If you remove just one item at a time, he may feel less separation anxiety.

Penny Warner

My son went through something similar. I think it's twofold: One—your son is very creative and sees value in recycling things. Two—he becomes attached to things he likes and doesn't want to get rid of them. Let him continue holding on to things that he treasures unless they can be passed on for better use, then explain to him how his clothes help other children. Perhaps save one or two of his favorite shirts, or make a quilt out of his old clothes as a treasured memory. Then, when he's done with something or has forgotten about it, go through his stash and toss out anything that is obviously used up, discarded, or attracting ants!

Steven Kairys

Your son shows some signs of obsessive-compulsive problems. Are there other behaviors or activities that also hint at such a problem, or are the wrappers and clothing the only issues? Consider consulting your pediatrician.

Q My children, ages five and six, will not listen to me unless I threaten to hit them. I do not like to hit, and I would like for them to listen to me without having to repeat myself one hundred times.

Mark Viator

Strong-willed children can be a challenge; they will constantly test boundaries. It's so important that you establish clear, concise, reasonable boundaries. You need to explain these boundaries to your children and make sure that they understand them. Let your children know that if they break these expectations, they will immediately lose a privilege or incentive. Be sure to find privileges that mean something to your children, such as playing with friends or their favorite video games. I recommend that a privilege or incentive be taken away for a twenty-four-hour period. If they follow the rules, then they get to keep their privileges.

The main point is to remain consistent. If you give in, sway from your rules, or allow them to team up against you, you are no longer being the guiding parent. If you remain consistent and follow through with the loss of privileges for not following the rules, then your children will understand that you have set the boundaries and that they will remain consistent. Remember, the more you play into their game, the more they will push and push the boundaries.

Naomi Drew

How frustrating it is when our kids don't listen. First of all, please know that you are truly not alone. One of the biggest complaints of parents today is kids not listening.

You are right in trying to refrain from hitting. When we hit, we reinforce hitting and aggression. Over time, hitting becomes less and less effective, as does yelling. What else can you do? Here are six steps you can take immediately:

1. Get to the root of the problem. What do you intuitively believe is at the heart of your kids' defiance? At the end of the day, when the house is quiet, put your feet up, have a soothing cup of tea, and ask yourself this question. Our internal wisdom reveals itself in quiet moments. Trust your gut. At the root of the problem could be jealousy, resentment for lack of time with you or their dad, or problems or conflicts going on in your home. See what rings true for you. Write it down, and journal about it. In the process of writing, other insights unfold. Insight equips us to handle the problems that confront us.

2. Talk to each child individually. First express lots of love. Give hugs and affirmations. Tell your child what you love about him, and be sincere. Kids see right through our words if they sense the slightest tinge of insincerity. Then, give an *I* message such as, "I feel very frustrated when you don't listen. I don't like yelling and threatening. How do you feel when that happens?" Listen to what he has to say, and reflect (paraphrase) his words. Ask your child why he thinks the defiance is going on. Keep listening and try not to interject opinions or judgments. The more you listen, the more trust you will build.

3. After speaking to each child individually, have a family meeting. Start off with hugs and some verbal expression of love. Have markers and chart paper at hand. Ask your kids for their help in solving the problem. Ask, "What can we agree to do so there's not so much yelling and punishing in our home?" Discuss this together, then write down the best suggestions they

make (along with your own). Ask them to suggest consequences also. Kids are more apt to honor rules and consequences when they have a hand in setting them. Some effective consequences may include time-outs, loss of privileges, reparations (owing you a set amount of time in chores for the time wasted in arguing or defiance), or loss of objects (video games, toys).

4. Follow through on what you say. If the rule is that there is no arguing, and the consequence is no TV for two days, then stick with it unyieldingly. Each time we back off, we reinforce the negative behavior.

5. Spend at least fifteen minutes a day with each child individually. This is absolutely critical. Parents have reported back to me that doing this improves discipline tremendously. By spending exclusive time, you send the message that your loving presence is something your child can depend on. If jealousy is an issue, spending individual time can be the cure.

6. If you do all of the above and the defiance continues, consider engaging in some family therapy. Doing so is a sign of wisdom and strength, not defeat. Nipping the problem in the bud now will prevent larger problems from happening later.

Barbara Gilmour

A very wise person told me when I was raising my two daughters that the first time we reprimand a child for doing something wrong, it establishes that the behavior was unacceptable. The second and subsequent times we have to address that same behavior, that child has not only done something wrong or displeasing to us, but she is now being defiant. Once I understood this, it was easier to enforce whatever type of discipline I chose to use.

The key here, I believe, is not the style of discipline you choose but that you are consistent in enforcing it. Five- and six-year-olds love to challenge you, and if you threaten them with a punishment and then don't follow through, they will persist until you cave. They will easily figure out how far they can push you. If you let them win in the small battles, you will regret what happens with the bigger battles later in their upbringing.

Q My five-year-old son recently started kindergarten. I am getting reports from the teacher that he is not listening to her, the lunch aide, and others. This same situation happened last year in preschool. I met with a child psychologist who suggested that we create a daily report card for my son that the teachers would complete. Each day they would put a happy- or sad-face sticker on activities letting me know how my son behaved. I don't believe that worked well because my son felt very defeated about not ever being able to do well enough. The psychologist then suggested that my son simply look to the other children to see how to behave. I was concerned about that as well since he would lose his sense of self, and in the long term it may be the wrong message about following others.

Penny Warner

It's normal for a kindergarten child to have trouble paying attention, listening, and sitting still, and it takes some children longer than others to learn these skills. I think positive reinforcement works better than negative. Instead of the teacher catching him not paying attention, perhaps she could focus on each time he does pay attention and could make a comment about it, such as, "I like the way John is listening!" It also may be that your son is not ready for kindergarten and that another year of preschool or a repeat of kindergarten might be advisable. He may need that extra time for his brain to mature.

Vicki Panaccione

In all this intervention, has anyone tried to figure out why your son isn't listening to adults? In what way is he not listening? Is he blatantly defiant? Is he having trouble hearing them or understanding verbal language? Is he developmentally delayed and perhaps not capable of the behavioral demands of the school setting? Do you have this problem at home, or does it only occur at school? My suggestion is to find out why the behavior is occurring before trying to create behavior management programs.

Then—and this is extremely important—any behavioral program that might be devised needs to be basic enough for your son to experience success. If it's a behavioral program that is needed, break his day into small enough increments to be able to catch him being good at least some parts of the day. Reward him for one smiley earned at any point during the day, and gradually increase the number of smileys he needs to acquire to earn a reward.

Simply leaving him to watch the other kids is no kind of interventional strategy. It's all right to encourage him to look to the other kids for cues as to what he should be doing, but that should not be the sole strategy. Have your child checked out by his pediatrician—and find another child psychologist!

Tina Nocera

Hold on a minute. You met with a child psychologist who suggested you get a daily report card from the teacher? Sorry, but I don't know too many adults who could handle that kind of scrutiny. Imagine if you went to work every day knowing that someone would report on your every move! No wonder your son felt defeated. Who is good all the time?

I am very concerned about the psychologist's suggestion that your son look to other children to see how to behave. Two major concerns come to mind: First, your child has a personality, and this advice is telling him not to be himself. Second, telling him to do what other kids are doing says that he should be compliant. But, what about ten years from now when other kids are making bad choices? Should he still look to the other kids?

Your son is a five-year-old who acts like a five-year-old. Please be patient and give him time to mature.

Q Like many toddlers, my son is very honest. How do I explain to him he needs to be gracious and thank people for gifts, even if he doesn't like them?

Barbara Gilmour

Isn't it a shame we have to teach a child that their honesty isn't always acceptable? If only their innocence could last forever. However, that is not how our world operates. As children grow and interact with others, it becomes necessary to teach them empathy, how someone else feels. This isn't an easy concept to teach, and it isn't one learned overnight.

The underlying problem here is getting the child to think not of the gift he was given but to have him think about the feelings of the giver. Not an easy sell. Prior to gift-giving occasions, prepare him with some role playing. You can pretend to be Grandma, bringing a gift for his birthday. Emphasize the time, effort, and even money Grandma expended for him. During this time, role play with a stuffed animal Grandma's reaction when he responds with appreciation and when he responds with a negative attitude. Overact being sad, unhappy, maybe even crying at the stuffed animal's negative response; and then overact being happy and excited about its positive response. Be sure to stress the importance of not hurting Grandma's feelings. You may have to do this several times for him to understand that we don't say something that will hurt someone's feelings.

Because the toy is of primary importance to him, let him know that if it is a toy he already has, it can be exchanged for something else. However, he still needs to thank the giver graciously. When he just doesn't like the gift, practice with him to say something such as, "Wow, that is really cool!" Or, "Thank you for getting me a gift." In that case, he should show gratitude for the effort shown by the giver.

Vicki Panaccione

It's funny that we want kids to be honest, and we encourage them to use their words, and then they get in trouble or we get embarrassed when they do exactly what we have taught them! Toddlers are generally honest, sometimes painfully so. If someone is fat or has stinky breath, they'll let you know that just as easily as they'll tell you how pretty a flower is. To toddlers, it's all the same. They call it as they see it.

In the case of gift giving, it can be hard to be gracious when the gift is something the child does not like. And it's not wise to encourage kids to lie about their opinions, either. Best-case scenario is to find something that can truthfully be said, for instance, "It was nice of you to give me a present!" Just understand that this is really difficult for a child to do, particularly if he is disappointed or confused about the choice of gift. In that case, it's up to you, his parent, to explain to the gift-giver that you appreciate the gesture and you are working on helping your child learn to be more gracious. Your child will learn to conduct himself as he watches you conduct yourself.

But a word of caution: Please do not consider the gift-giver's feelings as more important than your toddler's. Too often parents get embarrassed and end up scolding their kids for speaking their truth; this is very confusing for kids. Instead, take your child's developmental stage into consideration, and explain to the gift-giver what you are trying to teach. The adult will get over the awkward situation more quickly than the child who does not understand what he's done wrong.

Tina Nocera

Being grateful is something we can begin to teach very early. You might want to work with your toddler to make a gift for someone. As your son makes the gift, you can discuss how he feels and how thrilled he is to give the gift. That will help him understand how nice it is to give a gift and how much he appreciates the joy he gets when the receiver accepts the gift. Before his birthday or a holiday, you could remind him how good he felt and that others feel the same way.

Q My five-year-old son loves toilet-talk. Nothing is funnier than a poo-poo or bum joke. And if he finds it funny once, you can bet he'll find it funny twenty more times. How do I get him to tone it down?

Norman Hoffman

Children have a difficult time differentiating the lines that should not be crossed if parents change the rules. For example, if a parent joins in on the fun with the child, and later scolds him, the child will be unable to tell when it is all right to joke around. Therefore, I suggest that parents create firm boundaries about when something is funny or not. If it is allowed the first time, then it should be permitted the second time and thereafter. Your child may be more difficult to tone down and may need firmer rules.

Pamela Waterman

Don't get mad—I know, it takes patience! Say sweetly (through gritted teeth), "We don't say that in this family. Do you want jelly on your peanut butter sandwich?" He'll probably try the words forty times, but when there's no reaction, there's no fun. If he won't change the subject when you tell him to, say, "I'll decide for you," and go on with what you're doing.

Another possibility, but only if this works in general, is to say, "Big boys don't talk that way—they use real words," and remind him of what you prefer he say if he actually needs to use the bathroom.

Barbara Gilmour

This might be one of those things that ignoring is the best strategy for stopping it. Right now, he is getting the message from you that what he is doing is upsetting you. Sometimes negative attention is fun for kids this age. If you don't make a big deal about it, he may stop. There are a lot of cute books out there that contain this type of material that you might consider reading at bedtime. Or, create a special potty-talk time. This would let him know that he can talk this way but in a controlled environment—controlled by you. You could encourage him to play with action figures in his room, letting him talk this way. If his potty talk is no longer forbidden, it may lose its appeal.

Lastly, I would let him know that there are specific consequences to using this kind of language when outside the home or when guests are present. Be consistent and enforce your consequences.

Q My five-year-old doesn't listen well to instructions in school. I have tried preparing him each morning about being a good listener, but it doesn't stick. The teachers feel he is behaving badly, but he really gets excited about the activities and just isn't good about the strict rules such as staying in line and so on. I understand he has to comply, but I also get it that he is only five. How do I deal with this? I'm not sure if I am asking about dealing with my son or the school.

Vicki Panaccione

First of all, it is not clear whether "not listening to instructions" means he is not paying attention, he is deciding not to do it the teacher's way, or he is not able to follow the instructions. For instance, he can listen all day long to the instruction to color in the lines, but he simply may not be developmentally ready to do it! That is not what I would call not being a good listener—he may be doing the best he can. You and the teachers may be missing the real issue.

If, in fact, he is able to follow instructions and is capable of doing what is asked of him, it still may be a developmental issue that he's not ready for such formal instruction. Just because a child is five years old and the state says he is ready for school does not mean that he actually is ready. Kids develop at different rates; your son may need a little more time to mature. Don't push him any faster than he can go.

On the other hand, if he is simply not willing to follow instructions, you might need to work closely with the teachers on developing a behavioral program to reward him for compliant behavior. Be sure that the academic expectations the school is setting up are realistic for your child—not for five-year-olds in general but for your child in particular.

Christine Hierlmaier Nelson

You are not alone. My daughter has had the same challenges of following rules in school. The great thing about twelve years of school, though, is that our children get continued practice at listening, keeping their hands to themselves, following instructions, and treating others with respect.

I would practice things at home that your son's teachers say that he needs to do at school. Make a game of follow the leader, and let him lead sometimes, using his most serious and quiet behavior. Practice giving him two simple instructions, and ask him to follow through on those activities. Make sure you have his attention with good eye contact, and ask him to repeat what you just said. It may be that your son has trouble with natural focus, with so many distractions in a classroom.

Rather than allowing the teachers to label him as a troublemaker, ask them how you can work together to improve his focus. Ask his teachers to let you know when he is doing something well so you can reinforce that good behavior at home. And give it time. My daughter has learned a lot in the past year of kindergarten and does not have the same disciplinary issues she once had. She is still very social and chatty, but she has learned to follow the teacher's instructions. Practice and praise make a difference!

Tina Nocera

It might be good to help him practice listening skills at home. You might even tell him how you are trying to help him listen better, so you are partnering with him rather than scolding him. The following tips will help:

- Use a tone of voice that is respectful and calm yet firm.
- Do not give too many directions at once.
- Clearly state the directions in simple terms with reasonable consequences if they aren't carried out. Then, if necessary, carry out the consequences.
- Prevent confusion. Do not give directions in the form of a question or favor unless that is what you mean. I often hear parents say, "Would you like to

clean up your toys?" Why would a child want to do that? Simply say, "Please clean up your toys."

- Make sure that your child is paying attention and that there are no distractions when you are giving the instruction. If there is a TV on, turn it off before you give instructions.
- If you don't think your child heard or understood, ask him to repeat what you said so that you can clarify.
- Use positive reinforcement when he carries out your instructions.

Brenda Bercun

Is your son a good listener at home and in other social situations? Does he follow instructions and direction? Does he cooperate? If you have answered yes to these questions, then perhaps the school is asking for different behaviors or he is reacting differently at school than at home or other social situations. I encourage you to speak to your son and explore with him the differences between school and home regarding his ability to listen, follow instructions, and cooperate.

I also encourage you to meet with the teachers to discuss the details of the negative behaviors they are observing. Be prepared to ask questions about when they are noticing these behaviors. Ask for their thoughts about why the behaviors are occurring. Ask them for ideas to improve the situation. Perhaps the school's expectations are different from yours.

If you have answered no, then perhaps it would be helpful to encourage your son to listen under your tutelage. There are wide ranges of behaviors that are acceptable for five-year-olds. Some children are more active, impulsive, and excitable than others. Not every five-year-old finds it easy to stay in a line, sit in a circle, or wait her turn. In a traditional school, these abilities are required to promote a cohesive classroom environment. Create a positive feedback system to encourage your son. Catch him doing things well, and compliment his cooperation and patience. Support his growing maturity by letting him know that he is learning, and provide him the opportunity to do things better. We never want to quash a child's excitement, but we do want to support his ability to cooperate, learn, and socialize.

Q I have two sons, an eighteen-month-old and a four-year-old. Neither sleeps very well. The four-year-old wakes early, runs into my room, and makes loud noises until he wakes his brother and me up. (He also does this during the toddler's naps—even though he and I are doing something special during that time.) I have tried talking to him, explaining that we all need our sleep and that if he wakes early, he should try to go back to sleep so that he can feel rested for the day. I have pointed out days where he has gotten great sleep and how the day is so much more wonderful for him than on the days that he is tired. I have told him that waking people up on purpose is not fair. We have created a special morning box with quiet toys and books that he selected. He has no interest in this and charges into our room immediately when he wakes in the morning. I have brainstormed with him about what he could do if he wakes early and we are still asleep. While we may come up with ideas, he doesn't implement any of them. I have explained that he is not listening and that this (along with not hurting people or things) is one of the two rules in our house. I have told him if he doesn't listen when I ask him to be quiet the next morning, there will have to be a consequence. Taking a special toy away does not work. Taking a special privilege away has not worked so far. I am exhausted. Any ideas?

Brenda Bercun

It seems that you have definitely done a very good job at trying to solve this issue with your four-year-old son. It appears that he has taken control of the family's sleep schedule. I am wondering what his need is that causes him to be unable to allow the family to sleep. Is it a power struggle? Is it a need to feel connected to you in the morning? Is it that he knows once his baby brother awakes from his nap you will be going to the park or he will play with his brother?

I believe that consequences need to be related to the act. If he is unable to allow you to sleep in the mornings or come into your room and lie down with you so that you can sleep more, then perhaps you might be too tired to play games with him, take him on that special outing, or make his special meal or treat. If he wakes up his brother, then perhaps the plans that were going to happen when his brother awakened don't happen. If your older son is too tired because he didn't have enough sleep, then he may need to go to sleep earlier that night and miss out on a special family game, cartoon, or other evening activity.

Reinforce all that you and he have discussed to help him be more cooperative in the mornings, and let him know the consequences if he doesn't follow through. I urge you to keep the related consequences so that lessons are learned. When he does follow through and no longer wakes his brother, I would encourage highlighting the activities that you are now able to do because he cooperated. This will help him learn the power of cooperation.

Janet Whalley

My first suggestion is to find a book or two on sleep. One that seems popular is *Healthy Sleep Habits, Healthy Child* by Marc Weissbluth, MD. Also, there are many wonderful books about child development that might help you understand your son's changing feelings and behaviors. Here are a few more thoughts and ideas that I have learned from experience.

1. Your four-year-old son should be able to control his morning behavior, even if he can't control his sleeping schedule. To help him get enough sleep to keep you both happy, he may need to go to bed earlier. This may seem counterproductive, but it often helps with sleep issues. You may need to go to bed earlier, too, so you get enough sleep in case he awakens you in the morning.

2. It seems that your older son does not want to play alone in the morning.

He may feel that you and his brother are doing something together, and he wants to be part of it. In her book *The No-Cry Sleep Solution*, Elizabeth Pantley suggests that, once your younger child is past eighteen months old, you can put both boys in the same room for sleep. I know it seems scary, but because my boys were close in age, I put them in the same room in two cribs when the youngest was about one year old. It took a while for them to get used to it, but soon when one woke up crying, the other one would stay asleep. It might take some creativity to have them go to sleep at different times, but it can be done.

3. You could try some additional ideas to keep your older son busy and content to stay in his room until the right time. If you think he is hungry, you could put a snack (a small bowl of cheerios) and a drink (in a sippy cup) in his room for him to have when he gets up. You could use an alarm clock that is set for the right time to awaken you. It would be helpful if you drew a clock on a piece of paper that would show what time he is waiting for.

4. You could try a rewards system, such as a chart with your sleep rules on it. Put a bright sticker next to the rule each time he follows it. The chart may have rules such as the following:

   ■ Stay in your room until the alarm sounds.
   ■ Eat your snack if you are hungry.
   ■ Play quietly with your toys and books.
   ■ When the alarm goes off, come in to mommy's room for a big kiss.
   ■ Stay quiet when your brother is sleeping.

You could also use the silent treatment (suggested by Weissbluth) and return him to his room each time he awakens you too early. Best wishes with your sleep challenges. I know it will get better with time. Speaking as a mother and now a grandmother, parenthood can be challenging, but the memories of the joy and happiness last longer than the memories of the problems.

Trish Booth

I think there are two issues: his coming in and waking you up, and his loud voice.

Regarding his waking you up—four-year-olds are still working on self-control. When long explanations and choices don't work, try a simple rule with immediate consequences. It may be easier to refocus this as an issue of when he can leave his room. During his bedtime ritual, tell him that he can't leave his room in the morning until a special light comes on. Set up a light on a timer that will turn on about fifteen minutes later than the time he typically comes into your room. Explain that until the light comes on, he needs to stay in his room and play quietly. You can suggest he play with the toys in the quiet box. Explain that if he comes into your room before the special light comes on, you will take him back to his room. If he resists and makes a lot of noise and wakes up his brother, he loses special time with you when his brother is napping or some other privilege.

Then, the next morning carry through with the plan. Return him to his room if he comes in ahead of the light. Don't spend time trying to win your son over with reasoning. Expect some testing for a few days until he realizes that the new rule will stick.

When your son stays in his room until the light comes on, lavishly praise him. You can also consider adding a reward system of stars leading up to a tangible reward such as a small toy or special treat at the end of the week. After he has been staying in his room for about a week, you can slowly extend the time he must wait until he wakes you up. Remember, however, that he has his own biorhythm, and young children tend to get up early.

As for his loud voice, many energetic and enthusiastic children have loud voices. Getting your son to have a more appropriate volume may take quite a while. If his loudness is a result of his personality and not a hearing loss, aim for establishing a gesture that reminds him he needs to talk more softly. When his voice is too loud, touch him gently on his shoulder to get his attention. Then, in a soft voice, tell him to talk more quietly, and put your finger to your lips. When he lowers his voice, praise him. Over time you will be able to get his attention by using the gesture alone. As your son gets older, he will be better able to judge when he is too loud. Until then, you may have to use this gesture many times a day. In addition, you may also want to invest in a white noise machine for your younger son's room. This will help block out the sound of his big brother's voice.

Naomi Drew

Does the eighteen-month-old sleep in your room? If so, that could be the crux of the issue. Your four-year-old could feel left out of the mix. Even though you've provided him with wonderful alternatives, he may still want to be with you, too. In terms of waking his brother from naps, it sounds like there may be some jealousy happening here. Sometimes an older sibling will do things like you're describing out of resentment. It's normal and something your older boy will likely grow out of. Have you tried spending exclusive time with him outside of the house? Is there someone who can watch the baby while you and your four-year-old go for a walk or do something fun that's just for him? If so, this may help alleviate the problem. Fifteen minutes of exclusive time each day with your four-year-old is ideal. Also, allow him to vent. Ask him to tell you honestly how he feels about having a baby brother. If he says something like, "I wish I didn't have a brother," just nod and paraphrase what he says. Mirroring validates a child's feelings and helps him feel understood. Don't try to talk him out of his feelings. Whatever he expresses is better translated into words than repressed and expressed through aggressive behaviors. Let him know that you understand and love him just the same. As your eighteen-month-old gets older and the children are on more equal footing, their relationship will likely smooth out.

Q I have a very hard time getting my twin six-year-old daughters to pick up all the toys they've played with. But, at a recent parent-teacher conference, the teacher said she has no problem with my daughters at clean-up time. Help, please.

Tom Greenspon

We often hear how well our children behave in the company of family, friends, and school. That's great, until it sinks in that they're not behaving the same way at home. It could be they have figured out what they can get away with. For that reason, begin to clearly set rules and stick to them. Associate consequences to not cleaning up, and follow through on those consequences.

For example, tell them each day, "You will take all your toys, clothes, and so on and place them in the container labeled with your name, by the stairs. Each night, you will put all the items in the container away. If you don't, I will keep those items for a week."

Ellen Gibran-Hesse

I am assuming that you mean your daughters are inconsistent in cleaning up. In raising children, we sometimes hold them to higher standards than we hold ourselves. A little inconsistency is normal and can be overcome with making it into a game or a competition. Ask yourself if you are making this a rigid rule or if they simply need a bit of inspiration. Children will act differently in school because there are social consequences, and that is fine. Home needs a different approach. I made sure my sons got into the habit of making their beds and keeping their room in order at about age eight. A little slipping happens. When things got too out of hand, I offered to help. If they were overwhelmed, I made it a time to discuss organizing preferences and it also provided bonding time. I made it fun. As they grew, my help was seen as a bit insulting, but since I don't like big messes, they learned to keep a livable order for all of us. As college-age men now, they both are organized and tidy but not perfect. As my oldest son explained, organization helps him access what he needs quickly, and as busy as he is, that's critical. Come up with some fun competition; maybe the one who is done first gets special points, a special choice for an outing, or a choice DVD to watch. Let things go a bit. We all need to smell the roses even when we are young. Make organization a general trait to aspire to, and you will find that over time the activity will become a good habit.

Tina Nocera

Let's start with your twins' response to their teacher; it sounds as if she runs a well-organized classroom where the students understand their responsibilities and the consequences of not fulfilling expectations are clear. Your daughters are also motivated by seeing other children around them cleaning up. So try following this procedure at home. Make it clear that you are serious about your twins cleaning up after themselves, state the consequences for not following directions, and be sure to follow through. As any teacher will tell you, consistency and follow-through are crucial. Without these, you risk undermining your authority. And, just like those fellow students, you can set a good example by making sure that you always clean up after yourself!

Sharon Silver

Believe it or not, the best way to see if your children know the rules is to inquire about their behavior when they're with other people. Children feel safest at home. So, home is where they learn about refusing and not doing as asked. I think most parents would prefer that their children refuse them in the privacy of their own home instead of in public, don't you?

It might be helpful to watch how their teacher asks them to clean up in class. The teacher probably makes a statement that it's time to clean up and does no negotiating or reminding after that. The teacher relies on the established boundary that everyone must clean up what they're working on before moving on to the next lesson. That way, if a child doesn't clean up, the teacher simply redirects him to clean up his mess before moving on. That's a true natural consequence in action.

You can do that at home, too. You might say, "The TV only gets turned on when all the toys are back in the correct location. Call me when that happens, I'll take a look, and then I'll turn on the TV."

When parents get involved in the completion of a task, by using reminders, threats, and punishment, the task changes from being just a task to being an opportunity for power struggles or reacting to the complaining and whining. Let natural consequences teach them, and things will get done faster and with far fewer struggles.

Christine Hierlmaier Nelson

You are not alone. Many parents hear about good behavior and helpfulness away from home. Your children may understand your patterns rather than have an inability to perform tasks. If you tell them to pick up toys but are distracted by your own tasks at home, they may have learned to ignore you and keep playing because there is no follow-through. In school, there isn't a next activity until everyone performs the expected task, such as "No snack until cleanup." Plus, there is likely a game or song accompanied by the task in which all the children participate—so it is more fun. You may find that you have to supervise cleanup for a while until the expectation is set. Create a game of it. Tell them to pick up all the green toys first, then all the red, and so on. If they like competing with each other, tell them to see who can pick up the most toys by counting as they go. Set a consistent expectation, such as having them clean up the toys first, then you can go to the park together or let them play outside. This extra five minutes or so of supervised chores each day will help you establish a clear routine so you can get on with your chores, too!

Q How do you deal positively with a three-year-old who usually says no?

Pamela Waterman

Three-year-olds love to test their parents! They've discovered they have some choices in life, and they take every chance they can to try to be in charge. You have to choose your battles. When dressing the child, you can offer two choices of outfits you've already put on the bed. If she says no to both, you can say, "Show me the one you want from your drawer," and give in on that one. If that sets her off to picking out each piece one by one and wasting time, set a timer and say, "If you haven't picked one by the time the bell rings, I pick it." Then, stick to that. For other cases, you have to be firm and say, "Sometimes you get to choose, and sometimes Mom is in charge. This is one of those times when Mom is in charge," and again stick to it. Be sure to allow opportunities for her to say yes, too; then, offer hugs and say, "Good idea!"

Trish Booth

One way to deal with this behavior is to avoid asking questions that can be answered with no. For example, you can give the child a choice. Instead of asking, "Do you want to get dressed now?" ask, "Do you want to wear your red or your blue shirt?" This also lets you avoid saying, "It's time to get dressed," which can evoke a no. Any choice you offer must be acceptable to you. Your child may take a few minutes to decide—try not to pressure her for an answer. You may have to ask the question several times because your child may address the bigger issue and refuse to decide at all. Just pleasantly and firmly ask your question again. If you don't get an answer, announce that your child must not care, and say that you will choose. If your child asserts that she doesn't want you to decide for her, bring the discussion back to the choice of shirts. That should get her moving toward being dressed.

Another approach along these lines is to give your child a warning that an activity is about to happen or change. For example, you can announce that you are leaving the park in five minutes. Then, after a minute or so, remind your child's it's just about time to leave. Ask, "What's the last thing you want to do before we leave?" If you don't get a timely response, offer a choice between two activities your child might like. Again, this leaves your child in control of a small choice while you have control over the bigger issue.

Steven Kairys

Ignore the nos as best you can. Give a lot of praise for the times that your child is positive. Learn to give a few simple choices that are acceptable to you, so that the child learns to have some ability to control in a positive way.

Brenda Nixon

Rather than a discipline problem, what you probably have here is language development. Most youngsters say no because they're learning that the word has power. They are experimenting with many words. Expect to hear no even when the child means to say yes. Reading aloud to children is a wonderful way to expose them to many new words, plus it gives them that precious uninterrupted time with you that they crave. Another consideration: When a three-year-old says no too frequently, it may mean that she hears the word too often throughout the day as correction. If a child constantly hears no from adults, she's going to repeat it. If that's the case, use more directive words to replace your negative command. For example, instead of, "No running," say, "Walk." There's a chapter in my book *Parenting Power in the Early Years* that addresses using positive words to direct a child's behavior.

Q My three-year-old is being very rude lately. She is interrupting me while I'm talking to people or on the phone, and she seems to demand attention when I'm busy, even after I've spent one-on-one time playing with her. I would like to correct this behavior before she demonstrates it at nursery school. What is the best way to handle it?

Michelle Maidenberg

Three-year-olds exhibit some rude behaviors, but intrinsically they are not rude. If you view her as being rude as opposed to wanting something from you, you are bound to be less tolerant of her and her behavior. Some three-year-olds want their parents' attention all of the time, even during sleep time, when parents are on the phone, and so on. There can be adjustments to their behavior, but be aware that different children mature differently and their needs can change from one minute to the next.

When attempting to adjust the behavior, be aware of your reaction to it. If you're seeing her behavior as rude, you are probably becoming agitated and frustrated, potentially rolling your eyes, yelling at her, telling her over and over again to remain quiet, threatening to punish her, and so on. These are all very typical reactions. She isn't getting what she wants, so she's probably upping the ante, speaking louder and interrupting more often. Welcome to the world of power struggles. Unfortunately, three-year-olds often win and parents are left exasperated and feeling defeated.

A more effective way to handle the situation is to practice being on the phone with her. Slowly increase the increments of time where she needs to provide you with time to speak uninterrupted. Go from one minute to two minutes to three minutes, and so on. After she successfully gives you that time, reinforce her behavior with a reward such as a sticker for a sticker chart, a kiss, or a book. You can also pair the reward with positive accolades for her ability to hold out and some additional alone time where you are focused solely on her. You can also prepare something for her to do or play with when you are busy. For example, while she's waiting for you to finish your conversation, you can give her a teddy bear to play with. That way she associates the teddy bear with knowing that this will be time she will need to play independently.

Brenda Nixon

Bravo to you for wanting to correct inappropriate—albeit normal—childhood misbehavior. You may need a three-pronged approach to stop her: tell her during neutral times that interrupting you is rude and you won't tolerate it. If she interrupts you, do not give eye contact but touch her arm or shoulder so she knows you acknowledge her. Finally, wait until you are done talking to people and then immediately look at her to listen to what she says. Eye contact is a powerful way to show approval or disapproval.

Barbara Gilmour

I commend you for recognizing this and for wanting to correct these behaviors before she goes to preschool. It is our responsibility as the parents, caregivers, and educators to help children learn social skills. This is not something that is inborn or will happen overnight. They have to be taught to be empathetic, to care about others, and to be kind and respectful. The earlier we begin this training, the better for the child and for the adults around them. Interrupting is something all children do. When an adult does it, we wonder why they weren't taught basic manners. So, you are on the right track to tackling this problem now.

I have four tips for teaching children manners, no matter the social skill you want to teach them:

1. Training is introducing and demonstrating the skill.
2. Correcting is making sure the child understands the concept and repeating the steps until he does the skill with ease. This step includes modeling the behavior you want.
3. Disciplining is gently correcting and enforcing the use of the new behavior.
4. Encouraging is offering lavish praise every time the new skill is demonstrated.

Children want to do the right thing and please us. For them to be able to do so, we have to let them know the behaviors we want and how they can achieve them. Children the age of your daughter love play acting. I suggest using some dolls, puppets, or action figures to role-play the following skills to help her learn to not interrupt.

- Let her know ahead of time that when you are talking, you will raise your index finger and place it over your mouth to let her know she is to wait until you are finished talking.
- You may also train her to place a finger on your arm and say, "Excuse me," to let you know she wants to speak. In response, you should either put your finger to your lips to signal her that she should wait or tell her you will speak to her when you are done.
- With toy phones, practice what she should do when she wants your attention while you're on the phone. You can also have her get her toy phone when you are on a call, and she can role-play a conversation with her doll or puppet.

A great reward for learning a new skill is a new doll or puppet that is used exclusively for these role-playing activities to learn social skills. You are doing a great thing for your daughter by preparing her for new social situations. Recent research is supporting the need for social-competence training to help kids reject bullying. One such study of preschool-age children showed that those with social-skills training at this age performed better throughout their school years.

Q My three-year-old refuses to share at home as well as at school. Help!

Jill Wodnick

Developmentally, it is normal for a child to want to keep his own items. A role of parenting is to help children learn strategies to successfully interact with others. Refusing to share is all part of your child's sense of self right now. You can teach your child sharing through play, giving him opportunities to take turns and let you play with his toys. Make it fun: Try taking turns pretending to make banana bread by stirring the dough five times each. Try swinging a rope five times each then passing it along. The more you can make sharing and turn-taking fun experiences, the more comfortable your child will become with the concept.

Barbara Gilmour

This is normal behavior for a three-year-old. It's our job to help them learn that there are others in the world. We need to teach them to be kind, to care about others, to be kids that others want to be around. Empathy has to be taught. It doesn't happen overnight. Maybe that's why we get quite a few years to get the job done.

Use dolls or action figures to role-play behaviors that you consider acceptable and want the child to embrace. Introduce the behavior and model it so your child can see how it's done. Correct him as he is learning; offer praise when he does it right. He does want to please you.

If your child is having playdates at your house and there are special toys he doesn't want to share, suggest before the playdate that you put those special toys away until the other child leaves. Have your child choose some special toys that the other child can play with, and encourage him to share those toys. Introduce the child to taking turns. Try saying, "Let Sally play with your toy, and you can play with hers, then switch." When going to another child's house, suggest your child take a toy to share.

The more you practice this social skill at home, the more confident your child will be going into the school environment. Unwillingness to share won't be as acceptable there as it is at home. Your interest in improving this behavior now will have a positive effect on your child throughout the school years.

Ilyse Gorbunoff

Sharing is difficult at three. Children this age really don't understand that others have needs, too. I always found that a timer was helpful in teaching children to share. If your child wants to play with a toy and his friend does, too, tell each child that he can have the toy for five minutes. Set the timer and reinforce that when it rings it will be time to switch. Help the child who is waiting to find something else to play with while he waits. When time is almost up, give a warning that the timer will ring soon. When the timer rings, make the switch. Then, help the first child find something else to do. If he cries or gets upset, empathize and help him deal with it, but don't give in. Explain that when the timer rings again, it will be his turn. Also, spend time with your child talking about sharing, reading books, and teaching him about empathy, as well as how to be a good friend. It is a hard lesson to learn, but with patience and time your child will learn to share.

Derick Wilder

Not being able to share is a very common and normal behavior for a three-year-old, as it's a skill that is only learned over a long period of time. There are things parents can do to help the situation, beginning with setting a good example and taking every opportunity to show your child how to share.

Like many behaviors, this can be taught in phases. Start by having your child show a favorite toy to a friend and letting the child touch it. Next, casually ask your child to pass a toy to a friend. Even if it's not one of his favorites, repeating this simple act is a step toward turning sharing into a habit. During this process, make sure to praise your child with each positive step. In addition, you might want to designate a few toys as special and take them out of the room when other children are going to be around.

Q What is the best way to discipline a toddler? I hear so much about time-outs, but do they really work? I would love a how-to book on discipline.

Aileen McCabe-Maucher

Disciplining a toddler can be a challenging experience, but it is an essential part of being an effective parent. As both a professional psychotherapist and mother to a toddler, I like to think of discipline as a form of teaching. The first rule of thumb is to keep yourself feeling as grounded and loving as possible. Learning to manage your own stress through exercise, meditation, or "me time" is vital during your child's toddler years. Making sure that your own needs are met will make you a better parent and a happier human being. It is crucial to discipline a child out of love rather than anger. Hitting a child will only teach that violence is a way to assert power and control. I find that praising good behavior often prevents unwanted behaviors. Try to catch your child doing things right as often as possible. Setting boundaries with your child is a vital part of helping her learn and feel safe in her world. Ignoring unwanted behavior is a highly effective form of discipline. Keep in mind that discipline varies across your child's developmental abilities. Time-outs can be an effective form of discipline beginning around age two, or depending on your child's ability to communicate and understand verbal language. When your child exhibits an unwanted behavior, issue two verbal warnings. Keep your language simple and direct. If your child exhibits the unwanted behavior after two warnings, call a time-out. I recommend designating a particular spot in your home, such as a time-out bench or time-out rug. Remove your child from the situation, briefly explain the reason for the time-out, and direct or place her on the time-out bench or rug. When the child is in time-out, do not engage with your child in any way. Remove all of your attention from the child. I recommend giving your child one minute in time-out for each year of life. For example, a two-year-old should be in time-out for two minutes, a three-year-old for three minutes. When the time-out is over, ask your child to apologize and offer a hug or kiss. A toddler is hard-wired to test boundaries, and you, as the parent, are here to love, protect, and nurture her. This is a great question and shows you are committed to being a great parent.

Jill Wodnick

Discipline of toddlers is a balance of promoting safety, security, and play. I personally do not believe time-outs help redirect a toddler's behavior, but some parents need a time-out for their own balance. Understand that sensory play is the work of toddlerhood, so provide your child with something that is age appropriate as part of discipline. For example, while waiting in line at a library, I encourage you to have toy keys or another small toy your child can hold in one hand while holding your hand. Help your toddler deal with transitions, such as putting on her shoes, getting into the car seat, and so on by singing repetitive songs. Sing, "This is the way we buckle our belts," while putting her into the car seat. This will give her a consistent tonal pattern each time the activity happens. The tonal patterns of songs help regulate a child's experiences and promote discipline. And, make sure that your expectations are appropriate to the age of the child.

Brenda Nixon

Try to place yourself in your toddler's shoes. Toddlers are enamored with being in control and independent. They get angry when an adult thwarts their plans. They don't understand many of the words spoken to them, and they're often at a loss for the right words to express their emotions. They need about twelve hours of sleep in a twenty-four-hour period or their sleep-deprived bodies easily tire and they get in trouble for tantrums or being cantankerous. Because of their rapid metabolism, toddlers have boundless energy so sitting still is nearly impossible, or at least, torturous. And they do get hungry more often than adults, so provide small snacks throughout the day. They thrive on routine and like their days to be comfortably predictable.

Remember discipline is about teaching. Adopt an attitude of being your child's first and most important educator. When you correct your tot, be instructive and patient. Don't assume, "You should know better!"

Janet Price

This time in a child's life is all about learning what is hers and what is not, what she has power over and what she does not. It is also about needing assurance that she is safe and loved in the midst of exploring her ever-expanding world. Discipline for toddlers is more about guidance than punishment. Building that language between the two of you is essential. Telling your toddler "no hitting" or "use gentle touch" is fine, but do not expect her to necessarily understand and respond. As simply as possible, you can say the words you want her to eventually understand, and then redirect her. Redirection may be physically removing her from the situation that is encouraging the undesired behavior and placing her in another part of the room where there are new toys or activities that are more appropriate. Toddlers have short memories, and they can easily become refocused on a new activity and will forget what you took them away from. The bottom line is that toddlers need our attention and interaction. They have not developed enough internal controls to respond to what you tell them to do independently, even if they understand what you are asking of them.

You two will learn together how to have positive experiences and interactions as you honor what your toddler is trying to learn about in the context of a safe and loving home!

Ilyse Gorbunoff

The best way to discipline a toddler is to try to anticipate the problem and figure out what is causing it. If he wants to jump on the couch and that's not allowed, maybe it's time to go outside and do something physical. His behavior is showing you that he needs to get some energy out. When he is doing something you would rather he not do, just say no and distract him with something else. Save the time-outs for behaviors such as hitting or biting. If you use it too much, it does not work. Just keep time-outs short—a two-year-old shouldn't be in for more than two minutes, a three-year-old for three minutes, and so on. Use a timer so he can see how long he will have to wait. Explain to him why he is in time-out and how long he will have to sit. When you do use time-out, try not to interact at all. Ignore the crying and screaming, and stick to your guns. The most important thing is to be consistent. If you let him ride his scooter in the house one day, don't try to discipline him for that very thing a different day. A mixed message such as this will just confuse him. There is no one-size-fits-all when it comes to discipline. Do what works for you and your child.

Q My husband and I disagree on discipline. He was raised to believe that spanking is okay, and I don't believe it is. We have a toddler going through a normal bit of defiance, but the problem now rests with us disagreeing on how to handle it. I want to use time-outs, and he wants to lightly spank our son. Any advice?

Janet Whalley

As a mother and a grandmother of a toddler, I understand your dilemma. When I was a young mother, I thought that a light tap on the hand or bottom was okay. At this stage of my life, I think that spanking is not necessary to raise a cooperative child who is a pleasure to be with. Although some experts believe that spanking leads to violence, others believe that spanking doesn't always mean abuse. I suggest that you try some other discipline methods for a few months and see if you can get the desired results. Then, you can discuss spanking again.

First, you both need to talk about the behavior that is not acceptable to you, such as hitting you or other children; damaging your furniture, walls, or his toys; having a temper tantrum; or hurting your pet. Then, discuss what behavior is undesirable but sometimes is acceptable, such as being silly at the table, yelling loudly at the grocery store, or picking his nose. Of course, any dangerous behavior and activities should be stopped immediately.

Finally, you'll need to create a plan to stop the behavior and to teach him the proper behavior. Here are my thoughts on possible discipline methods other than spanking:

1. Change the environment in your home and yard so that there are fewer things that might cause problem behaviors. For example, remove items that could be broken or damaged by a toddler, or try changing his eating and sleeping routines, if they are affecting his behavior.

2. When your son does something you do not want him to do, use your angry voice and say, "No, don't do that." Be specific about what he should stop doing: "Stop pulling the cat's tail." Plan to give him two verbal warnings, and then move to action. (If he is doing something dangerous, loudly use your frightened voice, and move to action after only one warning.)

3. Move to action: Walk to him and say something such as, "Since you can't play with the cat without pulling her tail, you can't be near her now." Then, move your child or the cat.

4. Be consistent and persistent in your discipline. Sometimes it takes numerous times of showing your toddler what to do before he can learn how to behave. I remember that someone told me when my sons were young that it usually takes somewhere between six and six hundred times before they'll learn to stop doing an undesirable behavior.

5. You could try time-outs, but I think a toddler is too young for that approach to be very effective. Often moving him to another place or another room is all you'll need to do.

6. To control temper tantrums or other out-of-control behavior, I suggest that you try the technique of gently holding your child and saying, "I know you feel upset now, and I'm going to help you get control. When you feel like you can take control again, tell me. Until then, I'll help you stop yelling (or whatever behavior he is doing)." If your child has a temper tantrum at a restaurant or a store, you can use this same technique while you take him outside.

When I think of discipline, I think of teaching the right behavior, not just punishing the wrong behavior. Also, I believe that parents need to have clear guidelines about appropriate behavior and to teach their children what is acceptable in their home and family. A book that is helpful for parents of young children is *Love and Limits: Guidance Tools for Creative Parenting* by Elizabeth Crary. It is based on child development and gives different suggestions depending on the age of the child. I hope that this has been helpful and has made you think about options to discipline your son.

Steven Kairys

I don't think spanking works well. It is often done in frustration, rather than as a planned and organized response. Whatever you decide, be consistent and loving. Ignore what you can, and give immediate positive feedback and attention for the right behaviors. Try to redirect and give another chance before using something like a time-out. A star system for the right behaviors is often very positive.

Sharon Silver

Children explore everything they come in contact with. The world is filled with new experiences causing them to touch and play with everything; it's an unconscious developmental imperative. No matter how hard you try, you can't stop what adults often call "misbehavior," nor would you really want to. Misbehavior is how a child learns to behave. If you use time-outs or spanking to correct behavior, you're actually stopping more than 50 percent of the learning from occurring. Time-outs and spanking stop the back end of a child's learning by shifting the child's focus away from learning to focusing on the isolation of time-out and the humiliation and pain of being spanked.

Doing something wrong is how a child learns to do it right. Teaching, not yelling and punishing, is what allows a child to listen so he can hear your message. When a parent yells, lectures, spanks, or uses time-out as punishment, a child learns that his parents are the ones who hold him accountable. He doesn't have to hold himself accountable. Instead of learning how to be accountable, he learns how to bear the isolation of time-out, how to retreat from the intensity of yelling, and how to withstand the pain and humiliation of being spanked.

Understanding the concept of self-regulation, which is learned through trial and error, must occur before self-control can be expected. When a parent looks at correcting misbehavior from that point of view, it becomes obvious that time-out and spanking are adult reactions that interfere with learning rather than enhance it.

Q At what age should I teach my two-year-old manners?

Ashley Hammond

Manners are both taught and modeled. First, make sure that you know exactly what manners you want your child to have. Then, be sure to model them consistently and correctly. Your child is imprinting from you and others in her world every day, but at a young age you have the most opportunities to ensure that she learns good manners. Make the learning fun; for example, make up a little song related to closing her mouth while chewing, so she doesn't show the world her food. Be firm and enforce your rules, but like all teachers, make sure that you hold yourself to the same standard.

Eleanor Taylor

Socially acceptable behaviors are learned through experience. Children watch adults being polite and considerate. When they experience being treated the same way, they will tend to imitate these positive behaviors. Lectures don't work, but explaining gently and patiently what behavior you expect will move your child toward becoming (mostly) a well-mannered eater.

As soon as your child can sit at the table, it is important to establish appropriate flexible mealtime rules. Remember that young children can become restless sitting at the table too long. When your child shows signs that she is done eating, your ultimate goal is for her to ask to be dismissed. Children who start throwing food on the floor or having a tantrum are signaling that they are through (or tired or sick). When you remove the child from the table, do so with a gentle reminder that she is excused and won't be allowed to return because her dinnertime is over. You can give her an alternate activity, but it is best not to let her continue to eat away from the table. If she has not eaten enough food, plan to give her a healthy snack in an hour or so.

Be certain to include other household adults in your planning, because everyone needs to be consistent and follow the rules themselves. When expectations are repeated, it is amazing how quickly children cooperate. For more suggested family rules, check out the book *Feeding the Kids: The Flexible, No-Battles, Healthy Eating System for the Whole Family* by Pamela Gould.

And remember: there are no perfect families with perfect lives or perfect manners. Forgive yourself, accept occasional awful days or moments, and remember that children know when they are loved even when everything seems to be falling apart. Focus on doing the best you can and finding solutions that fit your current family needs.

Barbara Gilmour

Teaching manners should begin as young as possible. The first time you hand your child something, recite the magic words *thank you*. When the child hands something to you, say thank you back. When she is able to speak, encourage her to say thank you, and teach her that *you're welcome* follows. Do the same with *please*. Begin using the word routinely so the child associates that word with asking for something. When your child bumps into you or you bump into her, say excuse me, so she will learn that is the appropriate response. When she burps or toots, teach her that *excuse me* is the correct response. Do the same with *I'm sorry*. Children need to be taught empathy at an early age, so letting them know when they should say I'm sorry is important.

Saying good morning to family members or hello to neighbors, co-workers, friends, or your child's day-care staff starts the day on a pleasant note. At the end of the day or when leaving, use *goodbye* and *good night*.

Say, "I love you," every day. No one can hear those words enough. Don't ever assume that your family knows that you love them. The more they are reminded of that love, the more confident and secure they will feel. I strongly suggest that after disciplining your child, you hug her and say those three little words. It's important for the child to know that you disliked the behavior and not her.

As far as table manners go, start as soon as she begins eating solid food. You can keep your child's hands out of the cereal by moving the bowl out of reach. If she throws food, gently say no, and stop feeding until this stops. Introduce utensils as early as possible. Even though your child may not be able to hold a fork correctly, give her one that is size- and age-appropriate, and let her play and learn. When she has the manual dexterity to use it, demonstrate the proper way.

There are so many more tips for teaching your child manners that this could go on forever. Teach the skill you want her to master, model and correct as she learns, and praise her when she does it right. Rest assured that your child wants to please you and will make every effort to do the things that bring a smile to your face. The habits developed at young ages are the ones that remain with a child for life.

Q I have a two-year-old and a three-year-old, and I feel my life is one continuous no. By the end of the day, I feel really bad about that. I don't want my kids to remember me as that kind of mom. How can I break that habit?

Tina Nocera

It's a good thing you realize that this is something to be concerned about. The question is what kind of a house, family, and mom your children are going to remember. You get to choose, and one of the simplest things is to pause before you say no to things. Safety always comes first, but then don't jump to say no to everything. They are little and want to play, explore, and love their family as unconditionally as you love them. It is wonderful that we can build relationships with our little ones through play. So, find opportunities to play more because the fun is what they will remember, even if you've carefully disguised chores as fun!

You definitely have your hands full! Each of these ages can be quite delightful and challenging. The two-year-old is just beginning to discover his ability to have some control over his world. I am guessing that he is saying no to you just as much or even more than you are saying it to him. Three-year-olds are becoming more aware of personal preferences—what they want to wear, who and what they want to play with. I am also guessing that your two children act like twins at times, wanting whatever the other has and fighting for Mom's attention.

The good news is that you are already halfway there by becoming aware of the habit you have fallen into and wanting your children's and your experience to be more positive. Changing habits takes commitment and hard work, and you sound like you are up to the challenge! Without knowing the specifics of what all of those nos are in response to, here are some general guidelines.

Young children require consistency in their lives. That includes regular mealtimes and bedtimes. They benefit from routines associated with these important parts of their days. Children can become cranky, irritable, or overexcited when they are tired or hungry. The same can occur if they cannot predict when these needs will be met.

Young children need stimulating environments during their day. Both of your children will need supervision and some interaction from you during their play time. Depending on their temperaments, they may require more or less of your attention. Include the children when possible and practical in helping you. They can help you gather their dirty clothes for washing and help pick up their toys each day. Activities chosen by both you and by your children will keep their developing brains active and growing and will help provide a sense of accomplishment.

Being active is essential to growing bodies. Get outside as often as possible; spend time at the park or playground to let them use their never-ending supplies of energy. Active play lets them strengthen large muscles (running, skipping, hopping), coordination (climbing the jungle gym), and problem solving (how to get from one part of the climbing apparatus to another). There is often a social component when other children are present, as well.

Finally, try changing how you communicate limits. Instead of no, state the expectation: "Time to get ready for bed." Then, provide as much assistance as is needed, with the assumption that your two-year-old will need more help than your three-year-old. Redirection can help. If they are focusing on something that is off-limits, such as climbing on the furniture, state the expectation: "Furniture is not for climbing." Direct them to where they can climb, giving a verbal prompt, "The jungle gym is for climbing."

I believe that implementing some of these ideas can go a long way toward breaking your no habit, leaving you with much more time and energy to enjoy all the magic and wonder that your two- and three-year-olds have to share.

Derick Wilder

Children need and want to have boundaries set for them; it's one of the most important aspects of being a parent. At the same time, studies have shown that toddlers may hear the word *no* a staggering four hundred times a day. Here are a few suggestions to help get off the "no train."

Remember that even young children have a surprising level of comprehension. Giving a basic explanation when setting limits can help children better understand the situation, which in turn can relieve some of their anxiety. In addition, it can result in your children starting to see how to show empathy for others. You can also try to rephrase some nos into a more positive response. For example, "Yes, you can have a treat, right after we've eaten dinner." Or you can look for opportunities to give your children some control by offering them a choice, such as, "You may throw the ball in the front yard or on the back deck. Which would you like to do?"

Q How do you get a child who just turned three to follow the rules? My son, since he could walk, has been very destructive. He takes apart his toys and breaks things if they can be broken. We have not found what he values yet. He has gotten minor spankings, which don't faze him but for a moment. The same happens with time-outs and the removal of toys. I love him, and he is so sweet but is a handful. He is very different from his older sister. Any advice?

He is also very strong, and I think sometimes he feels like he can do what he wants because of his strength. To keep him from being bad I have to follow him around all day redirecting him. Trouble is just a few steps away.

Elinor Robin

He is who he is. Forget the comparisons; he is a high-energy, curious little boy.

- Give him choices, not rules: "Which pajamas do you want to wear to bed?" not "It's time for bed now!"
- Find ways to tire him out during the day.
- When he is not living up to your expectations, look him in the eyes and give him a choice.
- Never yell from another room. He needs your undivided attention.

Vicki Panaccione

Sometimes parents become so caught up in the problems that they find it hard to balance them with the positives. It's wonderful that you can still see the sweetness in him. It is not clear from your question whether the destructive behavior is related to taking things apart. If he has a real curiosity for how things are put together and, therefore, takes them apart to see, that is one thing. If he is simply being defiant and breaking things by throwing them, then that is another issue entirely. Let me address both.

If his behavior is driven by his curiosity or his interest in hands-on activities, then I wouldn't call it destructive, I'd call it explorative. In that case, I would give him things that he can take apart, and I would encourage you to work with him on putting them back together again. If they are his toys, he really has the right to take them apart, as long as he understands that it might mean the end of that particular toy. But, if he is less interested in toys and more interested in taking apart things, then I would buy playthings that meet those needs. You may want to try getting him to help you take things apart in constructive ways, such as taking groceries out of the bags, peeling carrots (with your assistance, of course), and taking clothes out of the washer and dryer. In other words, find ways to channel his exploratory behavior into helpful behavior.

On the other hand, if he is simply breaking things, I wonder what the root cause is. Simply punishing without understanding can definitely be futile. Is he angry? Does he not know his own strength? Is he inadvertently, but literally, being given too much power? Or, is he enjoying the reaction he gets from you for this behavior? Getting a rise out of you can be most entertaining. Be as calm and directed as you can be in dealing with this misbehavior. If he is in charge of where he goes and Mom follows, then the balance of power is askew. He shouldn't be dictating where you go—it's your job to direct his boundaries. Choose the room that you want to be in, and either contain him (with a gate, closing the door, and so on) or put him in an area in which he can be contained with toys and objects with which he can do anything he wants. Whatever you do, I would advise against spanking. Spanking is using your strength to exert power over him. If he is strong and oppositional, then he will begin to use his power in defiant response. If the above suggestions do not help, then I suggest consulting your pediatrician and perhaps engaging the services of a child psychologist who can evaluate the situation fully and provide assistance in developing effective behavioral techniques.

Jim Taylor

Sounds like quite a challenge. Of course, part of being a three-year-old is to test limits and cause trouble. And most kids grow out of this phase. Considering that none of your interventions have worked (and I would definitely not advocate spanking), it sounds like there may be more going on here than a simple behavioral problem requiring limits and consequences. Quite simply, it sounds from your description that he is out of control, not only your control but also his own control. I suggest that you have him assessed by a development specialist. His behavior may simply be a reaction to or a coping strategy for some sort of a neurophysiological issue. For example, the four-year-old son of friends of ours exhibited similar behavior. He was diagnosed with a sensory disorder in which he is hypersensitive to sensory input, causing him to act out as a means of dealing with his sensitivities. With help from a variety of professionals, the boy's behavior has improved dramatically.

Christine Hierlmaier Nelson

It sounds like your child has a very feisty personality. He is boisterous, prone to boredom, and very social. He probably likes having you follow him around as opposed to leaving him to play alone, so he tends to do things to get your attention. I liken his personality to a future entrepreneur or actor; he already wants to go his own way at a young age. Your job is to channel and exhaust that energy, which, unlike your older daughter, will require more energy from you. If you don't have a support system, look into early childhood programs and educators who can give ideas for getting time for yourself. In the meantime, find ways to help your son expend his energy. Is there a place he can run, jump, and play without danger each day? Can you set him up with fingerpaints, clay, or big blocks that can't be easily destroyed but will keep his hands busy? Can you give him opportunities to perform chores such as putting on his own shoes, setting the table, or helping you clean the car? Appeal to his need for independence and socializing with these tasks, but set limits in your routine. Naps and meals should always be at consistent times when possible. At night, calm him down with a warm bath, soft music, and a cuddle or back rub. Avoid sugar. He is already a ball of energy! When his behavior is either dangerous or unacceptable for the situation, it is okay to remove him and use a stern voice to show your displeasure. Give him time to calm down, then resume your activity or feel okay with leaving early.

Q My three-year-old son is energetic and spirited. Everything is a challenge with him. I'm having a problem teaching him to value other people's space. He just can't seem to stop getting too close to or touching people. For example, we were standing in a line and the man ahead (whom we didn't know) was chatting with us. My son took this as familiar I guess, and he started hugging this man's leg and getting silly. My son loves babies, but he just can't seem to stop touching, hugging, and kissing them, no matter how many times I remind him "no touching." I think he just doesn't understand why anyone would want this, so he forgets. I find myself saying, "Don't touch anyone," but that's not realistic either. Advice?

Ashley Hammond

It is the unconditional love and innocence of young children that makes them so special. You are right, however; balance, manners, and an understanding that people may not be as receptive to closeness or affection as he is is crucial. Like all behavior modification, a consistent message and enforcement of the rules is necessary. It is not unusual for young children to forget from one day to the next, and *never* is not a realistic timeframe for a young mind. Unfortunately, you will need to remain diligent and patient for a while longer, and he will eventually understand both your rules and, more important, why personal space needs to be respected. The good news is that this is normal behavior, and he sounds like a great kid!

Christine Hierlmaier Nelson

It sounds like your child has a spirited or what I call *feisty* temperament. A feisty child needs a consistent routine and parental expectations, as well as leadership opportunities to channel all of that energy. Stay calm and in the moment, one of the primary elements of patience that leads to good communication. What he also needs from you is an understanding of social expectations regarding personal space. Take advantage of his natural helpfulness and distractibility, and steer him toward a chore or activity when you are in public. Have him push a child-sized shopping cart or carry a tote. Keep his hands busy with a calculator or pad of paper and crayon. Have him pick items off the shelf for you and hand items to the cashier. Continue to talk to him about personal space. Give him alternatives, such as, "We pat the baby nicely," or "We say 'nice baby,'" or "We hold the baby's hand." Show him how to high-five or shake hands with adults rather than getting too close. Have him practice with you and a baby doll before you get into real situations. When your son gets too friendly, and it will happen until he takes on the new habits I've suggested, get down on his level and get him to look at you while you ask him to help you with a task or do another activity. This could be anything from holding your shopping list to showing you how he can stand on one leg or recite his ABCs. Be consistent with this process. Stay calm, redirect, and model good manners. Your son will soon catch on!

Trish Booth

Preschoolers have to learn to respect personal boundaries. That task is made more difficult when a child is energetic and physically expressive. There is no fix for this, but a combination of approaches and the normal developmental process will help. First, help him gauge personal boundaries by explaining that he shouldn't get closer to someone than the length of his arm without asking if it is okay. You can role-play that with him. You will also have to remind him of the arm's-length rule just before entering a public or play situation. Giving him a concrete and always available measurement will help him better understand the concept. It may not work a lot of the time, but using the arm's-length rule gives you an alternative to "Don't touch her." Toddlers and preschoolers often are overenthusiastic about babies. Rather than always saying, "Stop touching, hugging, and kissing," teach him one thing he can do to the baby. Try having him stroke a baby's arm with his fingertips or open hand. Have him practice on your arm and his own arm so that he knows how to stroke gently. Explain that babies like this kind of touch, and praise his gentle touching when he does it on your arm. Name the stroking "soft touch," "gentle touch," or something he comes up with. Then, before he can get close to a baby, have him show you what he is going to do. That way your corrections will be, "Only soft touch, no hugging," and "That's enough soft touching." Finally, your son may need or want more physical attention than he is getting. Throughout the day, before he gets wound-up physically, offer him a hug or quick snuggle. Model asking to enter his personal space and giving appropriate physical attention.

Michelle P. Maidenberg

Your son is three, which developmentally means he is naturally curious and attention seeking. He may even get overstimulated by touch. It's important early on to teach children about nonverbal cues and personal space, and it's never too late for them to learn these concepts. A way to accomplish that is to physically go really far away from him and then get really close to him. Get in his face, and ask him how that feels. If he can't find the words, provide them for him. For example, say, "Getting very close to someone or touching someone, especially if they didn't expect or ask for it, can feel scary or uncomfortable." Then, link that feeling to his behaviors: "When you touched the man at the grocery store, he may have felt the same way." I would ask him why he chose to grab the man's leg. Ask if he was trying to get his attention, make him laugh, and so on. Then, encourage him to come up with other ways to accomplish this. Problem solve this with him: "What other way, besides touching him, could you have made him laugh?" "Let's talk about ways we could get people to laugh without touching them and making them feel scared or uncomfortable." Also, teach the concept of nonverbal cues. For example, you may say, "Did you notice what the baby did when you touched her? Yes, she cried. When someone cries or pushes you away, what does that tell you about how they felt about being touched? It's important to notice someone's reaction to you touching them, and it gives you an idea how they felt about being touched." Your son could easily learn clues such as *no, stop, get off,* crying, wincing, and so on that communicate that he has to stop because he's causing the person discomfort. Assess with him how he might feel if someone touched him and he didn't want the person to touch him. This allows him to be in the other person's shoes and fosters empathy within him—an important lesson for all children.

Q My five-year-old is touching the other kids inappropriately. What can I do to get him to stop showing this behavior? It's really bothering me. Also, out of my three boys, he's the one who tries to push me to my limits by cursing and putting his middle finger up at the other kids. What can I do?

Christine Hierlmaier Nelson

I might need more information about this to answer your question, but I assume that your child has learned that this behavior gets the biggest reaction from you. Children learn to get attention either through "good" behavior or "bad" behavior.

Show your son that he'll get more attention for good behavior. When the boys are at each other, ask them calmly to stop and come to you. Tell all of them that you expect better behavior. Tell them to apologize to each other and say, "I love you." When they do that, smile and tell them you love them very much and feel so good when they get along. This action does not single out the bad behavior of one boy, but it does emphasize the importance of getting along as a group.

It may be necessary to repeat this several times or to change it up by saying, "Hey, I want each of you to say something nice about your brothers. Then, say something nice about yourself." Then you, as mom, also say something you like about each of them. It gives the boys the attention they crave from you in a healthy, positive way.

Janet Price

It is such a challenge for us as parents when our children act inappropriately. This is especially true when the inappropriate behaviors push people's personal boundaries or moral values, as the examples you have shared. My sense from your question is that your five-year-old reacts impulsively when frustrated and is unable to choose more acceptable ways to communicate what he wants, even if he knows what those ways might be. It sounds as if he hasn't learned appropriate responses in these situations.

It is going to be very helpful for both of you if you work at teaching him more acceptable behaviors to get the results he is looking for. Even if you feel that you have taught him appropriate behaviors, it is apparent that they are not in the forefront of his thinking when he is frustrated. Punishing him for not exhibiting skills he might not have yet is not helpful. Instead, remind him that kids do not like that kind of touching. Let him know when, where, and with whom he is permitted to hug, kiss, or whatever he is doing. Also, praise him whenever he does exhibit appropriate touch, so he starts to understand what is expected of him. When he curses, state calmly that he sounds angry. Then, give him more acceptable words to use at that moment.

The goal is to help him replace the strategies that he has become used to with more acceptable behaviors that can accomplish the same goals. Remember that learning new skills takes time. Try to praise him for any little steps he takes toward competence in these arenas. I wish you the best in this challenging situation. I truly believe that you and your son can turn this around to a more positive experience.

Vicki Panaccione

I understand that his behavior bothers you—as well it should! But, I want it to bother you not because it needs to stop, but because it exists in the first place. Basically, behavior usually is telling us something if we stop long enough to look beneath the behavior and identify the feeling.

A parent's first response is usually to deal with an inappropriate behavior by punishing it or trying to stop it in some way. However, while that's an important part of the intervention, you need to find out why the behaviors exist in the first place. While I don't want to alarm you, I think your son is crying out for help. It is unusual for a five-year-old to keep touching other people's private parts; that's very different from the normal curiosity of "You show me yours, and I'll show you mine." I think that he is or has been either touched inappropriately himself, or he is overstimulated from something he has seen or heard.

His cursing and middle-finger salutes are indicative of anger and the need to get your attention. He may be angry with one of his siblings for having touched him inappropriately or angry with you for not keeping him safe. Whatever the reason for his anger and sexual gestures, something is going on with him. The underlying problem needs to be identified and dealt with.

Try reflecting your observations to him: "I notice you seem very angry at your brothers (or Mommy). Can you tell me why?" Or, "You keep touching people's private parts, and it makes me wonder if someone is touching yours." If he opens up to you, great. If not, I strongly recommend seeking the evaluation and advice of a licensed child psychologist.

Brenda Bercun

It appears that your son is having difficulty with appropriate self-expression and socialization. Somewhere he has learned words and actions that express his frustration and anger in an inappropriate manner. Take the time to teach him appropriate expression with simple words such as, "I don't like that," "That hurt my feelings," " I feel left out," "I don't want to play anymore," "That makes me angry," "That frustrates me," or "That makes me sad." These expressions will help him in his development of emotional language and emotional intelligence.

I believe it is important that family behaviors set an example for each member of the family. Therefore, I would encourage you to promote a household where cursing and obscene gestures are not permitted from any member of the family. Modeling self-expression and emotions will help your son learn appropriate language when life is challenging.

In regard to his touching other children inappropriately, I encourage you to speak with him about good touches and bad touches. Help him understand that private parts of other children are off limits. It would be helpful to know in what context he is doing this behavior. Is it to evoke a response from the other child or the adults who are present? Is it causing children and parents to pull away from socializing with him? I encourage you to teach him appropriate touches such as high fives, a fist bump, or a hug when appropriate.

Help him to understand that the goal is for him to have friends who want to play with him and have fun with him. He will be able to have these good relationships when he is respectful, playful, and appropriately engaging.

Caregiving, Education, and Activities

Q How do I know if full-day kindergarten is better for my child than half-day kindergarten? Half-day is two-and-a-half hours, and all-day is six hours. Are there any parents or teachers who have had experience with both full-day and half-day programs?

Brenda Bercun

The decision to put your child into full-day or half-day kindergarten has much to do with the readiness of your child and your personal circumstances. Children who have been in day care five days a week for full days would probably do well in full-day kindergarten. Children who have been mostly home or have been in part-time day care may not fare as well.

If you are working full time and your child is already in a day-care situation, then having her in kindergarten half days and in a familiar day care the rest of the day might be an option. I encourage you to talk with your child's current preschool teacher or day-care provider to get her opinion on your child's readiness to be in school full time. How comfortable is your child being away from home for long periods? Does your child still nap? What are the needs of your family, and how would the choice affect your days?

I also encourage exploring with the school the school-day structure. What is the difference in the school experience for students who go half-days as opposed to the child who goes full time? Are both equally prepared for first grade?

A positive school experience is essential in the development of a child. Kindergarten is important for learning healthy school habits, socialization, and becoming part of a community. I respect your need for taking this decision seriously and wanting to make the best choice for your child. Sometimes it's difficult to know what the best choice is, and you need to trust your intuition.

Pamela Waterman

I'm a parent of three children, and I volunteered one day a week in the kindergarten of a parent-cooperative school. There are two main aspects to consider here: physical and developmental. If your child still needs a nap, stick with half-day. Tired children are in no mood to learn, share, or interact with others. On the other hand, my children were all high energy and stopped naps by age two; so, full-day kindergarten was a great outlet for their energy.

Does your child already know her alphabet, numbers, colors, animals, and other basics? Is she full of curiosity, ready to learn more? If so, she's probably up to the challenge of four or five centers of learning and projects each day. If she's not sure of the basics, half-day would be the perfect way to let her gain confidence in each of these topics. Then, she has time for unstructured play at home and with friends in the neighborhood.

Georgianna Duarte

Your question is an excellent one. The quality of all-day kindergartens varies across the nation. It is important to first visit, observe, and ask questions about each program. Quality factors include a child-centered curriculum, a safe and appropriate environment, stimulating and challenging activities, parent involvement, good teacher education, and a healthy social and emotional climate. Visit the program, and ask for information. Ask questions about each of the criteria, and spend time at the school observing.

> **Q** My daughter, who just turned five, is a perfectionist. She will do her homework over and over again until it is perfect. The teacher told me she does the same thing in school. We are very tolerant of mistakes, but I think this is just her personality. How can I help her be less hard on herself?

Jill Wodnick

I am curious about the type of homework a five-year-old would get and if it is very focused on fine-motor skills such as handwriting. You may want to adapt it so there are more gross-motor and creative expressions for her. Building with wooden blocks can show her the impermanence of a moment and the fluidity of the blocks going *kaboom* as they fall. Get her a large refrigerator box that she can decorate as a spaceship to harness her creativity. She will learn more of who she is through dramatic play and creative expression. These are portals in which young children learn about solving problems and dealing with differences. The more open-ended, play-based creative experiences she has with your encouragement, from playing with sand to making a leaf pile, the more she will rewire connections and patterns that reinforce less rigid outcomes.

Pamela Waterman

My oldest daughter was clearly a perfectionist by that age, too. She would spend hours on a drawing for school, when she should have been doing something else (like sleeping!). You're right, I think they are born with that tendency, even when you are tolerant and fair about it, but I feel for you, as it's not an easy situation. You can try setting a time limit (with a timer—it's nice and impersonal), telling her that you love how she works hard to do well on homework, but that other parts of her life are important, too. Make sure she has other activities, whether structured or not, that are not academic. Give her opportunities for just having fun, swimming, or taking a gymnastics or dance class. Let her do freeform art explorations, as in painting with shaving cream, where there are no lines to stay inside. And, be sure to point out times when you make mistakes: "Oops! I just realized I forgot to add the oil to these brownies. Oh, well, I can fix it" or "Well, this costume isn't perfect, but people will see it was made with love." When she's a little older, you might relate the story of Navajo rug weavers, who purposely put a mistake somewhere on every rug they create as a reminder that no one is perfect.

Ellen Gibran-Hesse

If you are tolerant of mistakes, your daughter may be suffering, even mildly, from obsessive-compulsive disorder. A good friend of mine had a son in grade school who suffered from it, and as with most people, did well with therapy. It is usually a fast therapy to desensitize the client. This behavior is not something you want to continue. Standardized testing is so prevalent and timed. She won't have time to get to perfection, so she needs to learn to let mistakes go. Consider getting her help before she encounters that level of testing in elementary school.

Christine Hierlmaier Nelson

Take it from a recovering perfectionist, this personality trait often stems from a fear of being wrong or criticized—the inner voice is already our biggest critic. To be wrong in front of others would seem devastating. Ask her what she thinks it means to be perfect and what it means to not do things perfectly. Get her to talk about what might happen if she turned in her work with uneven numbers or crooked lines, ideally with her teacher present so her teacher can back you up. Describe a time when you made mistakes and what happened and how you learned so much more from the mistake than the right answers. Give her an opportunity to be messy through art, playing in the mud, baking, or gardening. The chance to have open-ended experiences with no rules will help her see that nothing bad will happen if she doesn't color inside the lines. In fact, some of the most beautiful art, cooking, cures, and lessons happen in messiness and chaos! Have fun getting messy together!

> **Q** I have a six-year-old son, and he is showing signs of having attention deficit disorder (ADD). Although he really needs the help now, I realize that going through the process can take weeks, even months, to find the right medication. And, I realize that if I do choose to put him on medication, it will take a while to find the correct brand and dosage. How can I help him concentrate without having to put him through the process of getting him on medication?

Georgianna Duarte

Unfortunately, ADD is frequently mislabeled or misunderstood. Take him to two experts for clear and comprehensive evaluations prior to any medications. Seek time for family counseling to ensure that your own parenting skills are supported and nurtured and that the home environment intellectually, emotionally, and physically supports his development and is responsive to his unique needs.

Jack Marcellus

Please only consider medication as a last resort. Consider having a professional evaluation. I screen children every day who exhibit ADD-like symptoms. The truth is, there are usually underlying physical or cognitive barriers creating these issues. The eyes play a pivotal role in a child's school life. Many times the muscles around the child's eyes are not properly developed, which inhibits their ability to attend to tasks such as reading. This becomes a major source of frustration and can set off changes in behavior. Of course, many other factors, such as balance, midline, perception, and cognitive skills, may also contribute. Reading is so foundational to learning that if visual stamina is an issue, it can create problems across the board.

Mark D. Viator

Be sure that your son has ADD. Take him to a professional who can assess and diagnosis this properly. Do not assume that because he has some signs he has ADD.

If your son has been properly diagnosed with ADD or ADHD, and a professional has recommended medication, then begin that process. Yes, it is often a process of trial and error, but be positive about it and reassure your son that it will be beneficial.

Regarding other techniques that can help, the following are some suggestions:

- Do not overwhelm. Try to break down chores, homework, and so on into small, manageable steps. The more concrete you can be, the better it is for him.
- Focus on the positive. Let him do things that he is good at doing. Build upon these experiences, and that will help ease some of the frustration he may feel when he cannot concentrate.
- Use accommodations if necessary in the classroom. Because of the ADD, he may need a little extra time for some classroom tasks. Hold him accountable, but make sure that he has a fair chance to complete assignments and tests.

Q How can I tell if my four-year-old is ready for a team sport?

Ashley Hammond

Like all activities, the best way to find out is to try! Sharing (often a crucial part of team sports) comes to children at many different ages. Often, young children want the ball and don't want to give it up. This normal behavior is of course incongruous with a team sport and might be an indicator that they are not quite ready. Skill development, rather than team competitions, should be a priority. Working with many other kids with a similar ambition is good enough for the label "team sport" and should be what you are looking for. I strongly recommend exposing your child to a multitude of sports, both team and individual. Let your child explore different sports and activities. Keep it fun, and she and you will learn very quickly which activities she wants to pursue.

Derick Wilder

Many four-year-olds are certainly ready for some type of organized sporting activity. Most of the primary determining factors lie more with the structure and the goals of the sports program itself than with the child. You will probably want to do a little homework first.

I suggest looking for a sports program that is high energy, emphasizes fun, and provides ample opportunities for all of the children to participate. The programs should have chances to practice the various skills related to the sport, which will help build the children's confidence. At this age, the focus should be more on improving their motor skills and receiving positive feedback on their accomplishments than on a game score.

Tina Nocera

I'm not a fan of preschoolers in team sports because that might be too early for them to be attentive to the rules. I think it is better, if your child is showing an interest in a sport, to just play the sport with her. This way you are testing the waters to see how interested your child is. If your child is really interested (you will know this if she constantly wants to play or practice), then it may be worthwhile to find a well-run program.

> **Q** My husband is excited about getting our four-year-old son involved in a variety of sports. He has signed him up on a hockey team that meets twice per week and has enrolled him in skating school. Now, he wants to look into swimming lessons. Our boy just started pre-kindergarten, and I'm worried that school plus all of these new activities will be overwhelming for him. How much is too much at age four?

Derick Wilder

This is an increasingly common concern among parents, and there is a growing body of evidence to indicate that we have a tendency to overschedule children. With so many options, parents may not want to feel like their child is missing out on an opportunity. Let common sense and your child's enjoyment of the activities act as measuring sticks. If your son continues to enjoy going to his scheduled classes, that is a positive indicator. As a general rule, I recommend four-year-olds participate in only one or two organized activities at a time.

In this case, where your son has just started pre-K, he is being exposed to many changes in his life. I would let everything settle for at least a couple of weeks and see how he acclimates to all the activities before thinking of adding anything else to his plate.

Ashley Hammond

It is hard to say what is too much for a four-year-old, as they differ so greatly. Only you truly know his capacity to do multiple sports and a rigorous school schedule. The following are some warning signs of overload:

- He exhibits an unwillingness to participate in any of the activities. If he doesn't want to participate, honor his choice, as he either dislikes it or is simply too tired.
- He is unable to get up in the morning at a reasonable hour. Young children sometimes enjoy sleeping in but usually jump out of bed with vim and vigor. If your little one is always sleeping late, then he is too tired.
- He complains of soreness and fatigue, such as aching legs or a sore body. Soreness is not normal for a four-year-old and is a sign of overuse and too much going on.
- He is irritable and lethargic.

Listen to your child, and do not force him to do what he does not want to do concerning extracurricular sports activities.

Tina Nocera

I recently heard a great story from a friend. Her two boys were at the pool, where they were holding impromptu contests. She asked her six-year-old why he used the breaststroke in the race, which caused him to lose. He replied, "Wasn't this supposed to be fun?" Too often, parents are so excited about their children being involved in organized sports that they don't realize children are very happy to play with their friends without the involvement of teams.

And, what about your family time? The more involved your children are in organized activities, the less family time you have together. If your child likes a particular sport, especially at this age, nothing is better than a parent playing with him and coaching him in your own backyard. There is plenty of time for organized sports. Don't rush it.

Charlotte Cowan

The question you raise is an excellent one, and all parents and pediatricians wish we knew the answer to it. It is not obvious. Each child is different, and each child changes from one year to the next in terms of how much he can handle and what is appropriate for him. Seek the advice of your pediatrician, who knows you and your son well.

Not knowing you at all, my guess is that a four-year-old child who is in school five days a week probably would do well with one or two other activities. Children need unstructured time! If they are overstructured (and overstimulated), they tend to get whiny, anxious, and may even regress. Obviously, if you see any of these behaviors, cut back.

Consider simply offering your son different activities so that he can choose his areas of interest. He may prefer swimming to hockey. His passions need to be his own and not necessarily those of his mother or father.

Q Should I schedule structured activities for my three-year-old?

Ilyse Gorbunoff

A young three-year-old often has trouble adapting to structured activities. I would be careful in choosing them. Too much structure may cause your child to be frustrated and either become upset or rebellious. Joining the soccer team too young or not being able to follow the rules in dance class can turn a child off to those activities forever. You know your child better than anyone; it is better to err on the side of caution. If you think she is not ready, wait a few months before beginning. That being said, structured activities and classes are a great way to learn social skills and have fun with other kids. When you think your child is ready, look for structured activities that allow for movement and some freedom of choice in the activity. Gym classes or music activity classes are usually good places to start. Your child can learn about taking turns, thinking about others, and following rules while having fun. Also look for classes that you and your child can participate in together and where you can help your child adapt to more structured activities. At three and a half or four, your child may be ready to handle more structured activities, such as a dance class or a sport. Take your time—there's no rush to grow up. At this age, it's all about the fun!

Tina Nocera

If your child attends a preschool program, she is doing so to be social, learn to play with other children, and learn structured activities, which should be enough. At this point, you really don't want to put her in too many structured activities because she is young and should have plenty of time for free play. If your child doesn't attend a preschool program, then it is okay to put her in a program she shows interest in, such as music or gymnastics.

Derick Wilder

Three-year-old children are definitely ready for structured activities, as there are numerous benefits to be gained from them. If your child is not yet in a preschool or day-care environment, she can learn about following rules, communication, and building positive relationships with other children and adults through participating in a quality program.

A well-run program can also instill a variety of life skills, such as cooperation, respect, and sportsmanship. It is important that the experience be fun and positive, as it should be a building block for participation in future programs.

Structured classes for three-year-olds should typically be held about once a week, so the children maintain their enthusiasm. The classes should be high energy and not last more than an hour. Finally, remember that time devoted to unstructured free play is very important in a child's development.

Mark Borowski

Sure, structured activities are a nice complement to the free play that, I assume, she gets plenty of. If your child is in preschool, she's likely getting some of both each day. It's probably unrealistic to think you will model that routine on a daily basis at home, but try to schedule both at least some of the days. You might also try one or two weekly scheduled activities where your child is with a group of other children at a location outside the home, through art class, exercise, music activity, playdates, and so on.

> **Q** My son is twenty-one months old and takes "gym" classes every Friday at his day care. He loves it and comes home excited, trying out his new games. His teacher says he's terrific at it and quite fearless. What we love about his classes is the unstructured structure (if that makes sense) and the focus is on having fun rather than competition. Since my son loves this activity so much, should we consider putting him in one or two additional classes outside of day care? If so, what's right: a gymnastics school or one of these gym franchises such as Gymboree or Little Gym? I'm worried about these places being overly structured.

Pamela Waterman

I'm a big advocate of unstructured play. I'd say continue as you are for at least another year. If he's just gung-ho for more at that point, you could see what a gymnastics school offers for preschoolers. Even then, make sure it's fun first. In the meantime, perhaps you could do a playdate at your house with another child from the day care who could do the same kind of tumbling fun that they do at gym class. It's worth buying some cushioned mats to make a safe spot for this kind of play, even if you clear away the furniture and set them in the living room.

Steven Kairys

At twenty-one months, I would not add more classes. He is getting enough social time. He needs more time with you and his family. Too much time away from family distracts from the priority need for structure, love, and nurturance.

Brenda Nixon

At twenty-one months, your son is probably getting enough scheduled activity by going to day care. Don't fret about adding more to his life right now. You're right—tots need some predictability in their lives, but they do not need every hour and every day planned. They need time for spontaneous, imaginary, uninterrupted play. Keep up the good balance.

Janet Price

It can be so exciting to see our little ones begin to exhibit skills and strengths in various areas. Your pride and happiness in your son's enjoyment and abilities is apparent! As you consider whether to sign your son up for additional gym classes, think about his physical capacity to add more structured activities into his life at this time. Does he have energy to spare after his days at child care and on the weekend? If so, he should be able to handle another active class.

It is easy to overschedule and leave little time for a child to just be quiet and relaxed, with unstructured time for exploring in the backyard or playground, looking at books, staring at clouds, following his imagination, and investigating the world around him. It sounds like you have good instincts in this regard. I agree with your thinking about offering your son only one additional class to start, especially considering that he is still a toddler with many social skills yet to master.

Your other question, about what kind of gym program to enroll him in is also important to consider. At almost two years old, your son needs a program that will allow him to take much of the lead on what and how much to explore. Gym franchises geared toward young children offer a simple environment and structure that focuses on fun, exploration, and safety rather than competition. As your son continues to grow and develop, he will be more able to handle increased structure and expectations, such as what a gym school would provide. Also, as your son matures, he will be able to communicate more with you regarding how much ongoing interest he will have in formal gross-motor activities.

Have fun watching and supporting your almost-two-year-old son's enjoyment of exploring what his body can do with and without gym equipment and formal guidance.

Q I have been babysitting my grandson since he was three months old. Now his mother wants to put him in a child care center two mornings a week so he can socialize with other kids. I feel, at just thirty-five months, it would be traumatic to drop him off in an unfamiliar place with strangers. Am I correct?

Amy Sherman

Your concerns are understandable. However, your grandson is almost three years old, and that's a good time to encourage socialization. Furthermore, it's only two days a week that he'll be away from his usual routine. It seems as if you are feeling distressed about this because you may be losing your role or significance in the family. Just as you did with your own children, as they grew, you need to let go of your position with your grandson and let him interact with others to develop his natural independence and inquisitiveness. You will always be his grandma and have a special and important role in his life. At this time, it may be valuable for you to develop new activities with him that are unique to the two of you, so that your time together will continue to be significant as he gets older.

Brenda Nixon

At this age, it's developmentally normal—and healthy—for your grandson to have peer relationships. It's acceptable but not critical that he go to a child care center two mornings a week to socialize. He'll still have three full days with you.

Ilyse Gorbunoff

I know it is hard to imagine your grandson on his own in a preschool, but his mother is right. At almost three, it is time for him to start to learn how to get along with other children on his own. Before you know it, it will be time for kindergarten, and you want him to have the skills necessary for success. The fact is that most children attend preschool today, and those who do not may have a difficult adjustment to school. Two mornings a weeks is a great start to introduce him to what school is all about. To minimize his anxiety (and yours), work with his mother to look for a child care facility that will allow for gradual adjustment. Take him to visit a few times before leaving him. Let him meet the teachers and other children. On his first day alone, remind him that you are going but that you will be back. He may cry at first, but he will be okay. Call the school to check up on him, if you need to. Be sure to pick him up on time and acknowledge how proud you are of him. Before you know it, he will be accustomed to the separation and ready to have fun.

Q My child has an Individual Family Service Plan (IFSP). Both of us work full time, so his teacher in the afternoon is a different one from the teacher he has most of the day. How do I make sure we are being consistent with what his teachers are doing toward meeting his IFSP goals?

Georgianna Duarte

Request a meeting with both teachers and communicate your concerns, and be sure to come to the meeting prepared with your questions. List the ways you would like to see consistency maintained: records, observations, practices, verbal requests, and so on. Be sure to communicate that you truly are striving for a team approach in meeting these goals and objectives, and explore how all of you can keep this progress moving forward.

Vicki Panaccione

If you are not sure about how things are going, call a meeting! An IFSP is part of a system of special-education laws and is a legal document. The identified professionals must provide whatever services, interventions, and so on are stipulated in the plan. So, in your particular case, your IFSP should have clearly stated goals that are to be carried out by anyone who works with your son, whether it's in the morning or the afternoon. The plan should have specified procedures to provide opportunities for sharing between family and staff and among staff members. Keeping the lines of communication open is key to making sure that everyone working with your son is clear as to the goals of the IFSP and the role they play in helping him develop to his fullest potential.

Ilyse Gorbunoff

The whole idea of an IFSP is to create opportunities for learning interventions in everyday routines and activities. It includes interventions for different locations in a child's day. It requires consistency among all caregivers in order to be effective. You are right—communication between you and both teachers is essential in meeting your child's developmental needs. Ask the teachers if they would be comfortable sharing their email addresses with you. Create an email group where you can share ideas, discuss successes, identify challenges, and support one another. Some teachers like to text with parents so they can get immediate feedback. Also, see if you can set up a weekly or biweekly conference call. You don't have to be in the same room to communicate. However the information is shared, your child will benefit from the interaction.

Janet Price

Multiple professionals often provide services to a child with special needs. Your child's IFSP states both your child's strengths and his areas of delay; goals to work on throughout the life of the IFSP (one year); and which supports your child will be receiving, how often, and by whom. To monitor what each professional is doing to encourage progress, you can ask for regular feedback from each. This can be in the form that works best for you. You can try receiving a daily journal. This can be a wonderful mode for two-way communication between home and school. Each teacher writes briefly in the journal, and your son brings it home at the end of the day. You can update the teachers on any news from the home front that may be helpful for them the next day, such as your son did not sleep well and might be cranky or out-of-sorts today. Other modes of communication may include email, phone updates, or face-to-face meetings. You may use a form that states each goal for your child, with room for the teacher to respond to what was done that day to work on that goal. There can also be room on the form for anecdotes and news that might not relate specifically to one of the goals but is noteworthy nonetheless.

You can decide how often you would like to hear from his two teachers and can combine modes of sharing information. For example, you could request an email once a week and a meeting once a month. You and his teachers can decide the most helpful structure for receiving these updates.

Remember that you can always call a meeting at any time if you have concerns that warrant a formal gathering. At the same time, be sure to use this option wisely. Calling for face-to-face meetings when you could get the same answers via a phone call, for example, can be counterproductive to building and maintaining a positive relationship with your son's school.

I wish you the best as you continue this important job of advocating for your child to receive the supports he needs in the most consistent manner. Building a positive partnership with your son's providers will go a long way to making that happen.

Q The personality of my child's care provider and that of my child don't seem to be meshing all that well. How much time should I give the situation before looking for another care center? I hate to move my daughter and have her go through another round of transitions and separation, but I feel like the caregiver doesn't like my child.

Vicki Panaccione

Having differing personalities and not liking your child are two different things. Your child deserves to be in an environment in which she is lovingly cared for. If this center is not meeting her needs, you may have to switch. Before you do, however, I suggest that you speak to the caregiver to see how she really feels about your child and if there is anything that can be done to improve their interactions. Ultimately, if it does not work out, a change will be much less detrimental than leaving her in an environment in which she doesn't feel cared for.

Ilyse Gorbunoff

It takes time for the child, the parent, and the caregiver to develop a working relationship. However, don't ignore your mother's intuition. If you feel like something is wrong with this child care situation, do a little investigating. Start by talking to the caregiver and telling her your concerns. Share some of your child's admirable qualities, and see if she has other nice things to say. If she can engage in a positive conversation about your daughter, it means she cares enough to get to know her. This conversation may also lead to a relationship developing between the two of you that will help her become more connected to your child. If she can only share the negatives, such as, "She won't take a nap at rest time," then it might not be a great fit.

Get permission from the director to observe the class. Do this in the least obvious way; watching through a door or window would not be a bad idea. See how your child interacts with the caregiver and if your daughter seems relaxed and engaged. Does she seem happy? If you still feel unsure after you do all this, it's time to look for a new child care situation. It will be worth the transition if you are both more comfortable in the end.

Beverly Willett

It would be helpful to have more information. Has this happened before? How old is your daughter? How long have you given the situation? Is there any other stressor going on in your life that might be contributing to the problem? How long during the day is your daughter in day care?

I might say give it some more time if this has happened before or there are stressful situations at play in your life now. You're right to be concerned about uprooting your daughter, but that also depends on how old she is and how long this has been going on. I don't know whether you've sat down with the caregiver and talked about your concerns. That might be the place to start.

In the final analysis, however, I think parents should generally trust their gut. If you feel the situation is somehow harmful or could be, do what your intuition tells you to do. Dr. Spock encouraged parents to trust their instincts; I think he was right on.

Brenda Bercun

Is your child communicating to you that there is a problem with the care provider? Does your child appear happy and comfortable in this child care setting? Are your thoughts based on something that you witnessed or is it just a feeling that you have? If you have reason to believe that the current day-care situation is not a good fit for your child, then I do encourage you to first speak with the provider, discuss your concerns, and explore what can be done to correct the situation. If you are not satisfied with the outcome of the discussion, then I would encourage you to begin a search for a new provider. You may find that if the new provider is a good match for your child, the transition and separation may be easier than you anticipate.

Q We try really hard to maximize the educational opportunity for our child in every experience he has. How can I convince his teacher to do the same? She does some, but not as much as we would like.

Vicki Panaccione

Finding fault with a teacher is a very sensitive issue. You may want to offer your assistance to the teacher or volunteer in the classroom to be more involved in your child's instruction. Perhaps you can offer some resources you have at home when they study a particular topic, or explore the possibility of a class trip to reinforce the learning and offer to chaperone. Remember that your only concern in the classroom is your child; the teacher has a whole room full of kids who may have different learning needs, styles, and capabilities that make it difficult for her to do more.

You might explore whether your child would qualify for the gifted program at your school, where some extra enrichment is provided for very capable students. Otherwise, I suggest that you keep enriching him at home, and talk to the principal about the selection of his teacher for the next school year.

Elinor Robin

You are clearly a committed parent, and your child is lucky to have you as his advocate. However, the role a teacher plays is different from the role a parent plays. The teacher has to divide herself and her resources among all of her students. If you want to increase the percentage of time and resources that the teacher devotes to your child, you will have to make this happen. First, remember the old saying, "You catch more flies with honey than with vinegar." You will get more of what you want from the teacher if you find ways to show her that you appreciate everything (and anything) she does for your child. There are five methods you can use to show appreciation—physical touch, such as a hug or a pat on the back; sincere words of praise; performing a service for the appreciated person (cut down on the teacher's to-do list); spending time with the appreciated person; and tokens of appreciation (keep these appropriate, nothing that could be misinterpreted as a bribe). Next, clearly tell the teacher what your goal is for your child, and ask her to give you guidance about how you can accomplish your objectives. Keep her apprised of your progress, and value her as a key member of your team.

Georgianna Duarte

First, I suggest that you simply express to the teacher through writing and a conference that you consider the education of your child as not only very important, but also a team effort of rigor, attention, and commitment. Clear and respectful communication is so necessary in this relationship.

Ask for curriculum documents and ideas so that the communication is two way, respectful, and responsive. Before the conference is over, schedule the next two meetings to clearly communicate that you are quite serious about the progress and important experiences of your child.

Ellen Gibran-Hesse

You aren't specific in what you think is missing for your child or how old your child is, so I am assuming the child is grade-school age. The sad reality in most states is that teachers are overloaded with students and can't tailor education to each student. Most schools have programs for gifted children to enrich their education, and you may want to ask the teacher for programs that would benefit your child. If you can afford it, there are plenty of junior science or music programs, but it falls to you to try to find what will enrich your child. If your school doesn't have a gifted-child program, this is your chance to approach the school board and make it happen, which would make you a hero for many in your community.

Q My child is developmentally delayed, and I think the teacher focuses so much on preparing the children in her class for kindergarten that she kind of ignores my child's learning potential. For example, I've come in and the other children are in circle time doing an alphabet game or making up a group story, and my child is just wandering around the classroom. When I asked the teacher about it, she replied that my child couldn't keep up with the others. Should I just move my daughter to another school? Should I go over the teacher's head and complain to the director? Should I try talking to the teacher some more?

Vicki Panaccione

You should not have to change schools. There are state and federal laws that require schools to meet the educational needs of all children who have been diagnosed with any kind of handicap condition. If your child is developmentally delayed, there may be specific interventions and accommodations that she will require to best meet her learning needs. For your child to receive any type of special instruction, she must have a legal document that mandates the services she needs. There are two types of documents for children ages three to twenty-one that may be considered: A 504 plan provides accommodations within the classroom setting, such as special equipment for a physical disability or specific identified techniques that the teacher must use within the classroom to make sure your child is learning to the best of her potential. The other document is an IEP (Individualized Education Program), which identifies needed accommodations but also includes specific interventions within or outside the classroom, such as speech or occupational therapy, special education, small learning environments, a classroom aide, and so on.

There are various steps that you may need to go through according to the rules and regulations of your particular school district. If your child has not already been officially diagnosed, that would be the first step to take in making sure her needs are met. The school personnel or your pediatrician should be able to assist you in the diagnostic process. If she has been diagnosed already, then the people at the school board will be able to assist you in the qualifying process for a 504 plan or an IEP.

Georgianna Duarte

Communication with the teacher and school personnel is critical. Spend some time in the classroom observing so that you have an idea if this is an isolated incident or a recurring one. Communicate your concerns verbally and in written form, and ask for a team-responsive effort to foster the potential of your child. Once you have invested time observing and have summarized your observations, share these with the classroom teacher and reiterate your goals and expectations for your child. If not satisfied, take these concerns to the next level in the program.

Steven Kairys

A child who is having difficulties in the classroom deserves some individual attention. If a meeting with the teacher leads to frustration, then meet with the school counselor or school nurse. Your child may need an aide or may need a child study team evaluation if some beginning approaches do not work out. Do not get discouraged, and continue to advocate for your child's best interests.

Ilyse Gorbunoff

Differentiated instruction to meet the learning styles and abilities of all the children in a classroom is difficult, but it is essential in early childhood education. No child should be excluded from activities or made to feel like she can't keep up, especially in preschool! When the class is involved in activities that are not at the appropriate developmental level for your daughter, then modifications should be put in place so that she can be included. These modifications can be simple. For example, when playing an alphabet game, if she cannot yet identify the letters on the alphabet card, she could have the job of holding the card up for the other students. She would feel so proud to have this important job. I'm glad the teacher is not forcing your daughter to participate in activities that would frustrate her, but the teacher is also not doing much to make her feel like part of the group. It would be wonderful if your child could have an individual aide to assist her in the classroom so that her experience could be more inclusive. If not, ask the teacher and administrator if, perhaps, you could volunteer in the classroom when the class is participating in activities where your daughter may need some support. If after all of this you still do not believe that your daughter is getting the developmental support she needs, then it's time to look into a different school or teacher. You are your child's best resource, and there is nothing wrong in advocating for what she needs.

Q Our mornings are quite chaotic, and no matter how prepared I feel we are the night before school, we are stressed trying to get dressed, have breakfast, and get out of the house and to school on time. It is largely due to the dawdling of my three-year-old. I don't want to yell, which is a terrible way to start the day, but I am at my wit's end.

Jill Wodnick

You have identified a true stressor of your morning. What tasks are you asking your three-year-old to do, and are they developmentally appropriate for his age? While many three-year-olds are able put a shirt on, telling a three-year-old child to dress himself will most likely not work well. Put his clothes out in the area where you get ready, so you can supervise and assist him as needed. Consider brushing your teeth next to each other. To save a few minutes, pack nonperishables in the lunch boxes the night before, so you only have to add the perishable items in the morning. Identify a clear rhythm and routine: get dressed at 7:30, breakfast at 7:45, teeth brushed at 8:00, and so on. It is said that it takes twenty-one days to create a new habit, and leaving with less stress is a great goal. After twenty-one days, have a celebration for you and your child, and keep up the momentum of leaving in a grounded, balanced manner.

Ilyse Gorbunoff

The best way to avoid a stressful morning is to be prepared. It sounds like you have already attempted to do this. In the evening, continue to be sure that clothes are picked out, lunches are made, and homework and the backpacks are packed. Try to involve your three-year-old as much as you can in the preparation. Before he goes to bed each night, remind him of your expectations for the morning. Give him three jobs to do each morning because he is three years old now. Tell him that you are relying on him because he is a big boy and you need his help. In the morning, set a timer with him and tell him he has to finish the first job before the timer runs out. Help him if necessary to be sure he is successful. Try to make it fun, like a race against the clock. Be sure to give him lots of praise for his success. Then, do the same with the second and third tasks. Use a sticker chart for each time he completes a task. When he has ten stickers, give him a reward. Making him a partner in the morning routine may help him take some ownership of the process and make the morning routine a little easier.

Eleanor Taylor

This is a very real dilemma for most families, even those without a three-year-old. But, even the best routines will not help on some mornings when adults or kids wake up in a bad mood or can't find that lost shoe. Take the time to think about what your child needs and why your child is dawdling, then develop strategies to avoid stress. Some children need lots of time to wake up slowly. Others perceive when adults are rushed, and they overreact by feeling bad. One strategy that works is for adults to prepare for the morning rush by laying out clothes, packing lunches, or deciding what to serve for breakfast. Get up thirty minutes earlier than your child, to support your own need for a leisurely cup of coffee, dressing, and gathering your thoughts for the day. Consider making a picture checklist for your child to work through, with time to play (or better yet, play with you) at the end of the list. Each morning, set a timer for your dawdler and show him how it works. You'll be amazed that even very young children will pick up on the concept of hurrying to make room for play. The best part of having five minutes of playtime before you leave in the morning is that it sends everyone off feeling happy and loved!

Pamela Waterman

With three children under the age of five, mornings in our home could be a real challenge, especially because each child had a different personality that really came through at wake-up time! Here are some thoughts:

- Empty out the backpacks the night before, so you can see what needs to be signed for the next day or when money has to be sent in. For schoolwork, copies of field-trip info, and so on, set up a spot (use a magazine holder or an in-box) on the kitchen counter or desk where each child can place all the papers from school.
- If a child wakes up hungry, consider bringing him a glass of juice to get him started and preempt a bad mood.
- For the toddler, use a timer set to go off to let him know when to get dressed (after being up for a little and starting to play). The timer will serve as an independent reminder, instead of you being the one to crack the whip.
- Set out clothes the night before. If your child decides not to wear what you have laid out, offer one alternative outfit, but that is it.
- Keep bins with all their socks and stockings in a lower kitchen cabinet. My girls always came downstairs dressed but without socks and shoes, and so much time was wasted sending them back upstairs. Keeping the socks in the kitchen and the shoes by the door really saves time.

Hope these ideas help!

Q With all the technology that entices and surrounds our kids, how can I encourage my children (ages two and five) to love books?

Jill Wodnick

Balancing and blending technology and reading are important! Some ideas for promoting reading: Get library cards for your children and yourself. Try having a "stop, drop, and read" time in your home, for both adults and children. At your children's ages, storybooks on audio CD that tell your child when to turn the page are great for emerging readers and are a way of incorporating media. There are many short books and some longer books for kids on audio CD. Keep books in your home to promote literacy and school confidence; rummage sales are great sources for inexpensive books.

Ilyse Gorbunoff

Make reading something you do together! Spend time each day cuddling together and reading. Make a big deal about whose turn it is to pick the book or whose room you will read in. Visit the library or bookstore as a reward for good behavior. Let them see you reading and excited to get a new book. Expose them to others who like books and reading. Start a kiddie book club where everyone reads the same book, and then have everyone come to book club dressed as a character from the book. They can act out the story and, of course, have snacks. At the end of the book club, pick next month's selection. Each month do this at another friend's house.

Brenda Bercun

It appears that you understand the value of books to developing minds. Unlike television and movies, books allow a child to create his own images. Books promote language skills and knowledge in a different way than technology does. I do believe that both have their importance.

I encourage you to take a trip to the library with both of your children. Spend time in the children's section. Apply for a library card, and allow each child to bring home a few books. Of course, with a three-year age difference the choices will be different, which can be a plus. Your older child is probably just beginning to learn to read, and having her read to the younger sibling could be a great bonding and learning experience. Bring home a book that is above your older child's reading ability but is something you believe would be a good read, to give you an opportunity to read to your children. The more enthusiasm you show for books by taking the kids to the library, making time for reading, and talking about books, the greater the likelihood that they will develop a love for reading.

Christine Hierlmaier Nelson

First, read with them! Children this age love reading time with Mom or Dad, even for a few minutes. They will understand that books are important when reading is a regular part of the bedtime or naptime routine. Let them see you reading books and magazines, not just reading from your mobile devices. You could even work with them on making a handmade book, if you're crafty like that. Take them to the library and let them explore. Ask them to "read" you one of their favorite books to encourage early reading skills. At their ages, it's a perfect time to explore books together!

Ellen Gibran-Hesse

I was a reading tutor in elementary school and have always loved books. However, my sons had no love of books. They are grown and do well as readers, but they don't do it for recreation. I found with many of my students that instead of reading books, they did much better reading short stories and articles. At the ages of your children, it is important to read to them. My grown sons still cherish the books I read to them, and we took many a trip to the library.

Let me say one thing about technology: My nephew was in special education in school, and his spelling and reading were horrible. Once he started texting, however, his spelling improved dramatically, as did his vocabulary—enough so that he is going to community college today. So, don't be discouraged. The reality is that a love of books is a personality preference and can only be encouraged at best. I wish it were otherwise, as I love books.

Q I understand that my five-year-old twins are thrilled when school is out for the summer. But, I really want to make sure they don't suffer from "brain drain" while they are out of school. How can I keep them stimulated without taking away the carefree feeling of summer?

Georgianna Duarte

Play is learning, so engage them in social activities that involve play: enjoy community play days, museums, and the zoo. Work with them and set up a schedule of balanced activities that will respond to their needs, abilities, and interests. Your local universities, YMCAs, youth programs, museums, zoos, and libraries have many free programs, as well.

Mark Borowski

Scheduling a learning activity a few times a week should do the trick—trips to the library (or reading time at home), flash cards, computer games, board games, and so on are all simple activities that can be educational. Kids that age often like to help their parents do just about anything, so get them involved in whatever you do throughout the day, such as cooking, errands, and chores. Ask them questions about sizes, shapes, colors, distances—whatever you can think of to make conversation educational. Anytime you can make learning fun, kids will be more interested; so, don't lose the fun just because they're learning!

Tina Nocera

The summer is such a great time to learn and try new things. One of the ideas that worked well for me was engaging my kids in answering the question, "What do you want to be when you grow up?" We would explore careers that interested them and reach out to people who were in the profession, so my children could talk to them and learn what they did. The best part was that we were all learning together. We even got the chance to "work" in the profession. If, for example, your kids like animals and think they would like to be veterinarians, put them in charge of the care of your pet. If you don't have a pet, consider having them pet sit—with your help, of course. This summer activity can be a great tradition for your family and a way that you all can learn and grow!

Janet Price

Your worries are not without substance. In fact, research shows that, during summer break, all children do lose some of what they have learned. How much depends on how well they mastered the information during the school year. At the same time, you have good instincts about your children's need for a break from the formal process of academic learning during the school year.

I recommend that you do two things: First, try to let go of the need for your twins to remember everything they were exposed to in kindergarten. At the start of each new year, teachers review key information and learning from the year before to get a sense of who might need more specific relearning. Second, support their learning from the past year through fun games and activities, the key word here being *fun*. During the summer, you can play games such as counting the string beans you are preparing for dinner, playing I Spy as you look for anything blue outside, and finding objects around them that start with the letter *T*. In addition to your own homemade and spontaneous games, you can look online for ideas for educational games and activities that are appropriate for the age and abilities of your twins. There are excellent sites that keep children's brains stimulated through fun games. I recommend www.pbskids.org and www.turtlediary.com.

I wish you and your two children a wonderful summer full of fun, togetherness, and exploration. Happy summer!

Other Parents, Video Games, and More

Q How do I know if my child will be safe at someone else's house during a playdate? He is four.

Tina Nocera

It might be a good idea to host the playdate at your house first, and invite the mom to stay so you can get to know her. You might want to talk about your house rules regarding snacks (any allergies?), TV (it really shouldn't be on during a playdate), and always having the children in view to make sure no one gets hurt. The first time your child goes to the other child's house, you might want to accompany him so you can see firsthand that nothing presents a safety concern.

Janet Price

When our children are newborns, we take our responsibility for keeping them safe very seriously. The shift from total control for our child's safety to seeing him go off to preschool, child care, or playdates can be very stressful. Some of the people you allow into your child's world will have alternative lifestyles, parenting choices, and ways of being.

When struggling with these choices, it is important to distinguish between genuine safety concerns and others' choices that are "different and okay." You can take steps to ensure that the playdate environment appears safe by taking a look when you drop off and pick up your son. You will get a sense of both the physical environment and the social setting—is there a fence separating the play area from a busy street? Is the friend's parent friendly and welcoming, both to you and your son? Once your initial reactions are positive, you take another step toward letting go. And remember—your child will be a helpful communicator about whether he is feeling safe.

Pay attention to your son's mood both before and after a playdate. Ask him about what was fun at his friend's home and if there was anything hard about being there. Consider inviting the child over to your house for a playdate, as well. That can give you a good sense about how the two children play together, whether your son enjoys spending time with the friend, and what they like to do together. Do not push him for another playdate with a particular child if he does not want to go back again.

Be aware that your approach with your son to the playdate can influence your son's sense of ease. Our children are amazing observers, and they pick up, sometimes uncannily, on how we are feeling. If you are anxious about your son branching out a little in his world, you may be communicating that to him. That can result in him assuming that there is something about a playdate that is unsafe. By managing our own fears, we can send our children off to new experiences feeling confident, curious, and happy. I wish you the best as you welcome, with your son, these new social opportunities into his life. He is at a great age for making friends and spending time with peers.

Mark Borowski

By *safe* I'm not sure if you mean safe from abuse of some sort or just safe from physical accidents. This is an extremely important issue, especially if it's abuse you're concerned about. If there is any concern whatsoever about abuse, I would not allow the playdate under any circumstances. Period.

If your concern is about safety from accidents, I suggest you get to know the parents or caregiver of the other child before you allow the playdate. You can invite the child to your house first, have conversations with the parents, or spend time at their house during playdates before you leave your child there. You must see the inside of the house, play area, and so on and ask questions about what they plan to do. This is the perfect time to let the caregiver know of any rules or preferences you have for your child, and ask whether she can respect those rules.

Also, speak to your child ahead of time and give him some guidelines and permission to speak up if he does not want to do an activity or if he doesn't feel safe. You can give him the specific words to say such as, "I don't want to do that" or "My mom says I can't." Sometimes kids give in to peer pressure, but if you discuss this ahead of time and give him the words to say, it helps when those situations arise.

Ilyse Gorbunoff

The best way to be sure that your son is safe at a playdate is to get to know the other family. Suggest a playdate on neutral turf, such as a playground. As the children play, you can get to know the other parent and get a sense of how she interacts with her child, how she disciplines, how the children interact, and whether or not you would feel comfortable leaving your child with this parent. For the next playdate, invite them to your house so you can further develop the relationship. Finally, when invited to their home, go with your son. Maybe bring some coffee to share with the mom so you will have a reason to stay for a while. When you feel comfortable, leave for an hour or so. When you pick him up, talk to him about his experience. If he doesn't want to leave, it's a good sign that he was safe and had fun.

Derick Wilder

When you think about it, a lot of trust is required for a playdate. It is a delicate balancing act, as you have to feel comfortable that your child will be in a safe environment, but you don't want to be "that" parent who seems like she is policing other families. So the more knowledge you have, the better.

There are some reasonable questions you can ask the parents, to maintain your peace of mind without seeming intrusive. Find out what the children will be doing, which adults are going to be home, and how many kids are going to be at the playdate. Ask about any snacks and if the family has pets or a pool. The other parent should understand any concerns, as she'd probably have the same questions for you.

Q My first grader wants to spend the night with one of his school friends. How do I go about getting to know that family? I'm uncomfortable with him going until we meet. Am I being too careful?

Trish Booth

No, you are not being too careful. As your child expands his network of friends, it is important to know where he is going. That way you can both feel comfortable with his increasing independence. Perhaps, rather than starting with spending the night, suggest a playdate at your house. This can be a short time after school or a longer time on a weekend. This will give you a chance to watch them play together as well as to meet the new friend's parent. Before the playdate, think about what information you would like to know about the family. That way you can bring up these concerns when you talk with the parent during the drop off or pick up. Also, think about what you want to share about your son. If you don't feel comfortable with an overnight at the friend's house after this encounter, you can suggest the overnight be at your house. Then, try to get to know the other family better through a casual meeting or a shared adventure, such inviting them to come with your family to a park.

Mark Borowski

I don't think you're being too careful because you just never know. I think the best thing to do is explain to your son that when you have a new friend, you get to know him more first before doing something like a sleepover. Then, you can simply have the kids play together on several occasions, either after school or on the weekend.

You'll get to know the parents through the phone conversations, drop off and pick up, and by how their child acts while playing. You may want to invite the child's parent to stay during a playdate at your home. When you take your child to a playdate at their house, take the opportunity to strike up a conversation and stay awhile, if invited.

Another option is to be open about this upfront. Approach the parents and mention that your son wants to have a sleepover with their son, but you'd prefer that you all get to know each other a little first through playdates and so on. They might appreciate that.

Tina Nocera

You are not being too careful. But, honestly, if you ask most parents about sleepovers, the children rarely sleep. They often keep each other up all night, which results in a cranky, possibly sick child the next day. Perhaps you can consider a "sleep under," which is where the child comes home (in PJs) later than normal but does not spend the night.

Q My five-year-old daughter wants to have a playdate over. The problem is that I am not a fan of the little girl's parents and don't want to start playdates. How can I steer my daughter away without blatantly saying why?

Pamela Waterman

We had this situation with several families of my three daughters' friends throughout grade school. Sometimes I made a judgment based on how I saw that the parents did not keep track of where their child was during a school event; other times I'd hear the parents swearing at each other or just using behavior that wasn't right for our family.

I suggest that you arrange a playdate that is on neutral ground, such as a playground or park, where you can keep an eye on the children the way you want. Or, have the little girl to your house, but find an excuse for why your daughter cannot go over to the other child's house. If you really feel you don't want to have any playdates of any sort, you can fall back on the story that your family is so busy right now with school, activities, and so on that you're all just trying to keep a low profile for the time being—and maybe later this could work out. Definitely go with your gut feeling, particularly when there's a safety issue involved.

Vicki Panaccione

That's a tough one! You might skirt the issue by saying that you don't really know her mommy, but you are friendly with a mom of another of your child's friends. Then, suggest inviting that child over by saying, "You know what? I'd like to have a playdate, too. How about we invite Susie Q over because you're friends with her and I'm friends with her mommy? Then, we can both have a friend over!" At five years of age, that ought to appease her.

Janet Price

One of the interesting and often unpredictable aspects of our children becoming social creatures is whom they bring into our lives. Your daughter wants to have a playdate with someone she is drawn to. My recommendation is to honor her request. It sounds like your problem is with this child's parents. You do not need to invite them and can subtly communicate that by stating your pick-up and drop-off times.

As your daughter grows and matures, she may choose friends who have parents you have little in common with and might not choose to spend time with socially. That should not be your criteria for who she wants to play with. What will be more helpful for you is knowing what kind of playmate this child is–that is your focus as the mother of a child whose social interests are blossoming. Encourage social interactions that help your daughter build confidence as a social creature.

Remember, your daughter's friends do not need to have parents who are your friends or potential friends. By allowing her to have some control over whom she wants to spend time with, you let her grow as someone unique and separate from you. You have the opportunity to celebrate her choices and support her advances into the world of play.

Q I was looking out my window this morning and noticed a father walking quite a distance ahead of his little girl, who appeared to be about two years old. It would have been easy for the child to run into the street or for a car to hit her while turning into a driveway, since the little girl was so small. Should I have said something to him? We are all cautious of correcting other parents' behavior, but what if something had happened to that little girl and I didn't point it out to the father? In light of a recent tragic crash involving a mom who apparently was driving while intoxicated, I am taking the concept of accident avoidance more seriously. Your advice?

Ashley Hammond

Unfortunately, we all have different thresholds for safety. Equally, we all process advice and guidance from others in different ways. Unless the child was in imminent danger, it is hard to imagine a positive outcome through a verbal interaction with that particular parent. It is refreshing to know that guardian angels like you are around, and sometimes just being aware can be enough to stop a situation. We all have a moral and sometimes legal obligation to intervene in certain situations, but we cannot legislate everyone's behavior. Continued diligence and awareness are crucial, but try to remember that you will not be able to right all wrongs.

Charlotte Cowan

This is a great question that raises important societal and ethical issues. America is increasingly becoming a culture in which we are taught to mind our own business and to avoid expressing concern when witnessing an event that is illegal or dangerous or both. In the world of children, this includes playground, gun, vehicle, and water safety. In figuring out the right thing to do, you might consider the following: Is your obligation different if the person endangering a child is a neighbor, a family member, or a perfect stranger? Is your obligation different if what you see puts the child at risk for something unpleasant, such as being stung by a bee, or for something life threatening, such as walking into a busy street? These are questions that each of us must answer for ourselves. I have a big mouth where children are concerned. Of course, I am a pediatrician, and it is my profession and passion to keep children safe. My experience is that all parents worry about their children, too. My own answer to the above questions is to ask what the risk to the child is and whether I would want to be warned if it were my child. If I would want to be warned, then I put the child ahead of any concern about what an irritated grown-up might say to me. If, in speaking up, I have helped prevent a child's injury or death, then there is no question that expressing my concern was the right thing to do. My advice is to trust your instincts and speak up for those children who are too young to speak for themselves.

Tom Greenspon

This is a tough question and one that many of us are confronted with in one way or another. There is no question that this was a dangerous situation for the little girl and that the adult was acting negligently. Whether he was lost in his own thoughts, angry with her, or impatient, he was absent from his post as the adult in charge. I think we should all have the courage to say something in these situations. To remove some of the potential tension, you can start by saying you don't want to intrude and you are not meaning to be critical, but you are worried about the little girl's safety. In a tone that indicates you are addressing your concerns rather than trying to judge, you might mention that you are aware of too many accidents that occur to children and that you just want her to be safe. He might be grateful for the advice; he might also feel ashamed, bothered, or angry. If he ignores you or argues, you can simply say you just felt the need to say something, and then leave. You will have done the right thing, even if you can't control the outcome. These days, the village it takes to raise a child often includes strangers!

Jim Taylor

This is a judgment call. Every parent makes a decision, hopefully a deliberate one, on the rewards and risks of anything their children do. The difficult decisions are those in which there is a low probability of severe consequences. Do you play the low odds of something bad happening because the benefits outweigh the risks? Or, do you avoid even the low odds (and perhaps appear overly protective) because, if something does happen, however unlikely, you wouldn't forgive yourself? I must admit that I give my two girls, ages four and two, considerable latitude in exploring their world beyond my wife and me. I believe the benefits are significant: self-confidence, independence, and exploratory behavior. Of course, we set limits based on the environment they are in and the risks of harm.

Each parent has to decide her comfort level for her children's explorations (and I usually allow myself to feel a bit uncomfortable for the sake of their development). Certainly a child who is impulsive and could, for example, run out into the street without thinking needs to be supervised closely. Others who have shown good judgment can be given more freedom.

At the same time, if you see genuine danger, it might be appropriate for you to raise your concern to the father. The key is how you approach him. Confronting him with, "How could you be so irresponsible?" will probably not work. But, you could strike up a conversation with him that raises his awareness of the issue: "I notice that you let your daughter roam pretty far from you. I'm always curious about how parents decide how far is too far."

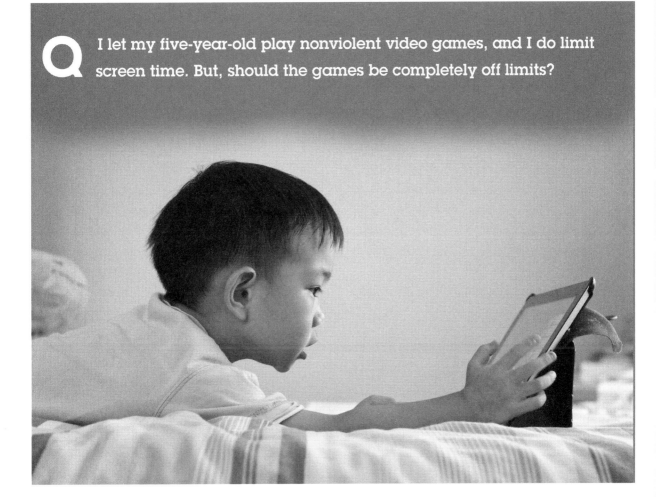

Q I let my five-year-old play nonviolent video games, and I do limit screen time. But, should the games be completely off limits?

Ashley Hammond

The research on the effects of video games on young children is at best inconclusive and has caused diametrically opposed opinions. Be sure to discuss the context and meaning of the acts in video games with your child. Ensure that he understands the difference between right and wrong. It is also crucial to respect the age warnings and ratings on the games. Facilitate activities away from the TV and video games to keep a good balance in his life.

Vicki Panaccione

This is the age of the video game. I think it's unrealistic to make them off limits altogether. It sounds as though you are doing the two main things I usually recommend: monitoring content and limiting the amount of playing time. Balance his play time with lots of other activities, such as outside play, drawing, building, and so on. As long as there is a healthy balance between video-game time and other activities, playing nonviolent games is fine.

Beverly Willett

I know it sounds cliché, but I really think moderation is key to most things. Still, you don't spell out your limits—once a day or once a week? And for how long? Whatever you do, I wouldn't give video games "special treat" status, for example, as a special allowance for good behavior. Treat the time you permit as no more significant than time for other endeavors. There's no such thing as too many books or too much time spent reading. If you allow video games, make sure you encourage a love of books. If your five-year-old is like my children and other children I've known, what he learns to love at five can have a great effect on his future. How does your five-year-old see you spending your time—with books or video games? At that age, you can influence what your child will come to love.

Mark Borowski

Generally, most activities are okay as long as they're within limits. Electronics are such a fundamental part of society and growing up today. Ask yourself if it appears your child is being adversely affected by the video games, and decide from there. Video games for entertainment are okay and games for learning are even better, so maybe you can incorporate some of those.

Q My son comes home from school and heads right to video games, which drives me crazy! It can be beautiful outside, but he just ignores the suggestion to play outside as if I'm not even talking to him. I am concerned, but that is all he wants to do. How can I stop this?

Vicki Panaccione

You asked exactly the right question: "How can I"–the parent in charge–"stop this?" You are in charge. You get to make the rules. Kids love video games. They are fun, exciting, and addictive. But, just like all the other rules you make about what he eats, when he goes to bed, and where he goes, you get to make the rules about what he plays, when he plays, and how long he plays.

Kids are going to ignore suggestions, because suggestions give them a choice. Rules, however, need to be followed. Your job as the parent is to set up rules about video gaming. If you want him to go out and get some exercise after school, then after school is not the time to play video games. Some families have a rule of no electronics on school nights. Others say no electronics until homework is done. Still others allow their kids to play for an allotted amount of time. The specifics are up to you, but the need for rules is clear. It will be a little more difficult for you to do this, since he is already used to playing when he wants to. Decide on the rules, tell him what they are and why they are being imposed, and stick to them! If he balks, limit the time even more.

Tina Nocera

It's really about balance. If he comes home and plays a video game for forty-five minutes, then he plays outside and gets his homework and chores done, that is not a problem. On the other hand, if you have to pry the game from his hands after he played it all afternoon and evening, that is a problem and one you can control. You can do that by taking the game away if that is necessary.

Many parents use timers, and that works well as long as you are consistent. Don't give in to pleas of "five more minutes" because it will easily become another forty-five minutes. Keep in mind that a healthy, well-rounded child gets a variety of activity and experiences, so playing video games isn't a bad thing if done in moderation.

Sharon Silver

I, too, struggled with video games. The truth is video games are part of our culture; insisting that your son stop playing them will only cause him to find ways to play them where you'll be unable to regulate his habits.

I wrote an article addressing this exact issue, "8 Limits That Make Video Games Good for Your Kids," on my website. I've included three important points here:

- The underlying principles for every video game are math, problem solving, and strategic processes. Those skills are all disguised as fun, so a child can easily master them, thereby advancing his thinking. Get involved in which games are being purchased without insisting on only academic games.
- Just because your child's peer group only talks about the cool, violent games doesn't mean that's all they're playing. Saying, "Try it, you'll like it," to get your kids to try an academic game doesn't usually work either. Create a rule that says, "In this house we alternate between games every other day." Make sure not to distinguish between academic and "cool" video games or there will be more resistance. If he's unwilling to rotate games, you can say, "I'm guessing you're too young to play and follow the rules. We'll put the game away today and see if you're able to alternate tomorrow."
- Video games are solitary and sedentary. To help offset this fact, do an activity trade. For every thirty minutes of large-muscle activity, such as running, cycling, or basketball, he earns ten minutes of video-game time.

Derick Wilder

Video games are both ubiquitous and addictive, so it's not always an easy task to wean children off them. You need to have a list of fun options ready to fill up his time.

You can arrange activities for your son and his friends, preferably based around being outdoors. Another option is to extend your son's video game into the real world, perhaps by encouraging him to draw or create the game's characters or come up with activities based on the game. Again, the idea isn't to completely eliminate video games but to limit the time spent on them by offering fun, creative, energetic alternatives. Also, you might want to spend some time playing the game with your child, which can be not only fun but also a bonding opportunity.

Q We went to dinner with family friends and the mom gave her son, age four, an electronic tablet to play with as soon as we sat down. I was taken aback because we just don't do that and see dinner as a way to help children learn manners and social skills. My son started asking me for my phone and I said no, but his friend was busy playing a game. Should I say something to my friend about not doing that again?

Eleanor Taylor

The primary purposes of sharing a meal are to eat nourishing food and to enjoy one another's company, and both are hard to do while using an electronic device. You were right to explain to your own child that the table is not the right place to use electronics.

Your friend probably has reasons for giving her son the tablet during dinner, such as worrying about his behavior in restaurants or wanting to distract him because he is very hungry. Next time you are meeting her, you might consider preemptively discussing what you'll be bringing to keep the children entertained before and after the meal, such as paper and markers, small toys, or some picture books. You could then casually mention your rule that your child must put all distractions away during the meal itself and ask if she is okay with that.

Rosalind Sedacca

It's not your place to say something to your friend about not giving her son a tablet. You can later explain to your son that you believe dinnertime is family time and don't agree about having kids play with toys during dinner. No two families will agree about all parenting decisions. Just be consistent and willing to share your perspective with your children so they understand and appreciate your values. That's all you can do.

Mark Borowski

It sounds like it bothered you enough to say something, so I would encourage you to do so. I think you could simply explain what mealtimes mean for you and your family and then ask if she can go along with that when you eat meals together. You'll want to position it in a way so she doesn't get defensive. You might even start the conversation by asking her to do you a favor. Or, just say you'd like to talk to her about something.

This could be just one of many differences in how you parent, so I hope she takes it well and can listen. It's really not that big of an issue, and people should be able to discuss simple things like this. If she overreacts or gets very defensive, it's likely an indication of how different your values and parenting styles are and can help you decide how much time you want to spend with them.

Q My six-year-old son loves to play outside with his friends. The problem is that he thinks he is big enough to play outside without being supervised. He would be very happy if he could ride his bike around the block and play ball on the street (our block is not too busy), but that isn't possible. I love the fact that my son loves outdoor play, but he thinks I'm babying him. Do any children get to play like that anymore?

Pamela Waterman

I believe in erring on the cautious side, no matter where you live and how wonderful the neighborhood and the other children. I waited until my children were eight years old before they could be outside without me right there. Even so, I checked on them out the window a lot! If you have a fenced-in backyard, you probably don't have to check on him as much, but front-yard play is just too public. It's a shame, but that's the way of the world. When they turned ten, I let my children ride their bikes around the block, though I set time limits. About playing ball in the street—I'd only allow that if you are out there to watch for cars, probably until age twelve. Even a quiet street can have some random teenager come whipping around a corner too fast, and the kids are watching the ball, not traffic.

Vicki Panaccione

Depending on your neighborhood, it may be perfectly safe for him to play outside. If all the other six-year-olds in your neighborhood are playing ball in the street outside your house, you might need to take a look at your own reluctance to allow your son to do the same. Sometimes our parental fears can get in the way of making rational, reasonable decisions. However, if you feel the need to supervise, let him know that this rule is not negotiable; if he wants to play outside, you will have to be out there also.

If he feels that you are babying him, perhaps he is embarrassed around the other kids. Or, perhaps there are things he is now capable of doing that you are not allowing him to do. Ask him what other things he would like to do, beyond playing outside unsupervised. There may be other ways you can begin to allow him to have some more autonomy that don't involve safety issues.

Tina Nocera

Start a movement on play! Why should our fears stop our children from having the kind of a childhood like the one you had? I'm not suggesting that your child should go outside alone, but he should be allowed outside to play. Get to know your neighbors (perhaps have a block party). In some places, local parks have play workers, usually education majors, who lightly supervise children but allow them to play in nonstructured activities. Can you encourage your community to start this kind of activity?

Derick Wilder

It's no secret that most of us were able to go out and play in our neighborhoods much more often than children do today. Rarely do we see groups of kids running unsupervised in a local park or riding their bikes down the street. But free play has numerous developmental benefits and is essential for children.

Several factors have caused this shift, including overscheduling our children with structured activities, an increased fear of stranger danger, and a perfect storm of electronic media options. Recognizing this allows us to start looking for ways to reverse the trend. A first step is to carve out time for our kids to play with other children, perhaps by starting a play group, either in your neighborhood or nearby park. And while abduction by a stranger is a parent's worst nightmare, the statistics show it's an extremely rare occurrence. So, do use great caution and find safe options, but don't let that fear paralyze you into inaction.

Q It's so hard to keep young children away from the news. My six-year-old saw news about the Sandy Hook school shooting and asked me if he was safe. I reassured him, but I am concerned that he does not believe that he really is safe. Quite frankly, I am concerned as well. How can I get past the fear and really comfort my child?

Tina Nocera

Shortly after the tragedy in Sandy Hook, a number of my blog readers wrote in with this very same question. Here is how I responded: I was driving on Rte. 95 North in Connecticut shortly after the tragedy and spotted a billboard that said, "Sandy Hook chooses love." Perhaps that is how we begin to recover—we choose love.

So they could begin to heal, the young students of Sandy Hook returned to school to familiar surroundings, thanks to thoughtful and intentional community support. They lit up when they saw their desks, book bags, teachers, and friends. Children are wonderfully resilient and always look for the good in people. They look to love.

We feel a deep sadness for the victims' families because we knew that it wasn't just this first Christmas they would be missing their children, but every Christmas, every birthday, every first day of school. There is an emptiness that won't end for the families.

We're also filled with fear that this could happen anywhere to anyone. When our children ask if they are safe, how do we honestly respond? How do we confidently send them off to school? I've thought about this a lot since the incident happened, and I have a couple of answers. Mr. Rogers suggests we look to the helpers. Fortunately, the good people in the world are in the majority. Though this speaks to our outlook, having a good frame of mind isn't enough. We need to make a difference, get involved, and be part of the solution to make needed changes to laws. This will demonstrate to your children that we are not victims.

Vicki Panaccione

This is a spectacular question and an unfortunate sign of the times. More than anything, your son needs to believe that he is safe. Kids need a sense of safety and security to be able to venture into the world. You, as a parent, owe it to him to provide that sense of safety. If you have your own fears—which are very understandable—you may want to talk to a therapist to develop stress management and relaxation skills for yourself. It is very scary to kids to know that their parents are scared. Your son needs to be able to lean on you with his fears and believe in your ability to keep him safe.

Now, that doesn't mean that you can't talk about how frightening that incident was. It was terrifying for all of us. But, you can provide your son with the best assurances you have regarding the safety of the area in which you live, the precautions that the school has taken, and the fact that there are thousands of schools and this was one incident.

One of the hardest things to do as a parent is to teach our kids to be cautious but not anxious. You want your son to be vigilant, but you do not want him to live in fear. Putting the incident in perspective—how many schools are safe and how his school is a happy place—will help to allay his fears. And time also has a way of calming things down. Give it time.

Janet Price

What a challenging time this is for us as parents. We want to do everything we can to keep our children safe, but there is so much happening all around us that is very unsafe. To make things worse, there are often events that we feel powerless to affect.

You are on the right track. Focus on how you can take care of yourself emotionally so that you can then help your child. Limit how much your child listens to the news.

Try to keep yourself calm. Your child will take his cues from you about how to feel about the tragedy. Give your child extra physical closeness and comfort; these acts of love and caring communicate a sense of safety to your child. Keep to your regular routines and structure. This will help your son know that the daily events in his life have not changed.

Ask him what he has heard about the shootings. Let him know that he can talk about the event whenever he needs to. Let your son know what you are doing to make the world a safer place for him, your family, and for other children and adults in your community, such as donating to an organization that is fighting for safer gun laws. By following suggestions such as these, you will help your son learn how to navigate this amazing, miraculous, unpredictable, and potentially dangerous world we all live in.

Mark Borowski

These days, I don't think we can be fearless and fully comforted. Crime can and does happen anywhere. The best you can do is to be informed and make good choices in any situation involving safety. Your spirituality can play a comforting role in these instances, for both you and your child. A strong faith and spirituality is an integral aspect to life, and it is never more important than in times of challenge, problems, and crises.

If you have specific questions or concerns about school safety, get them answered by the principal or school administration. You may also make some decisions about house safety and strangers and then discuss them with your child. Taking these actions will ease your own fear and help you comfort your child as well.

Index

3/27/18

Parent
306.874
NOC